Successful Supply Chain Vendor Compliance

The author validates what I have come to understand about most companies with respect to vendor management policies and practices, i.e. they are broadly substandard. This book offers a hard, candid look at why companies and vendors have not been more proactive about due diligence, and why plug-and-play SCM tools, while often impressive at creating efficiency and reporting capabilities, do not supplant the role of proper ethics, governance and communication in optimizing the vendor management relationship. The author serves as an educator as he defines for us what constitutes vendor management best practices and demonstrates how synergy in the vendor management process flow impacts profitability. CEOs, CFOs, IT auditors, and IT consultancies will gain tremendous insight from the author's observations and recommendations that translate well toward improving vendor management performance for company and vendor.

Andrew J. Tabone, Principal and Managing Consultant,
AJT – IT Talent & Vendor Management Advisory Group, LLC

Successful Supply Chain Vendor Compliance

NORMAN A. KATZ

GOWER

Published by
Gower Publishing Limited
Wey Court East
Union Road
Farnham
Surrey, GU9 7PT
England

Gower Publishing Company
110 Cherry Street
Suite 3-1
Burlington, VT 05401-3818
USA

www.gowerpublishing.com

British Library Cataloguing in Publication Data
A catalogue record for this book is available from the British Library

Library of Congress Cataloging-in-Publication Data
Katz, Norman A.
  Successful supply chain vendor compliance / by Norman A. Katz.
    pages cm
  Includes bibliographical references and index.
  ISBN 978-1-4724-7201-4 (hardback) -- ISBN 978-1-4724-7203-8 (ebook) -- ISBN 978-1-4724-7202-1 (epub) 1. Business logistics. 2. Management--Computer programs. I. Title.
  HD38.5.K383 2016
  658.7--dc23

                                                                                    2015028085

    ISBN: 9781472472014 (hbk)
    ISBN: 9781472472021 (ebk – ePDF)
    ISBN: 9781472472038 (ebk – ePUB)

Printed in the United Kingdom by Henry Ling Limited,
at the Dorset Press, Dorchester, DT1 1HD

Contents

List of Figures and Tables

Figures

Tables

About this Book

I have been involved in the technical and operational aspects of supply chain vendor compliance across different industries (retail/consumer packaged goods, pharmaceutical, marine, electronics, and book publishing) since 1993 and along the way I have had the opportunity to help two national trade associations in the United States with their vendor compliance initiatives.

From 2003 through 2007 I was the Supply Chain Consultant to the National Marine Manufacturers Association (NMMA, www.nmma.org) the largest marine industry trade association in the United States. In my capacity I provided technical and end-user documentation on the marine industry's electronic business-to-business (eB2B) platform; served as knowledge leader in meetings between manufacturers, retailers, and distributors; designed carton and pallet label formats and guidelines; and presented at various marine industry trade shows on the initiatives we were progressing.

From 2008 through 2011 I was a member of the then U.S. retail industry's 20-year-old trade association Voluntary Inter-industry Commerce Solutions (VICS, www.vics.org) as a member of its recently formed Trading Partner Alignment and Compliance (TPAC) committee. As of 2013 VICS has become the Apparel/General Merchandise sub-group of GS1US (www.gs1us.org), the United States entity of the global organization GS1 (www.gs1.org) which will be reviewed later on in the book. The TPAC committee was charged with trying to bridge the gap between retailers and vendors in the ongoing discrepancies and struggles of supply chain vendor compliance. One initiative of the TPAC committee was the establishment of industry-wide performance metrics that retailers and vendors would all agree to. The other initiative was borne from an idea of mine.

After my first TPAC committee meeting I had the idea of creating a set of supplier education courses that would teach new supplier entrants and existing disruptive suppliers how to be good retail vendors. The more educated a vendor, the less disruptive the vendor and thus the less costly the vendor to the overall supply chain, a win-win for both the retailer and the vendor. The President and CEO of VICS at the time, Joe Andraski, was passionate about the supplier education idea and I proceeded to develop a six-series suite of supplier education courses. At no cost to the retailers and for a small fee for the suppliers, the VICS TPAC supplier education certification would be recognized across the retail industry, at least (initially) by VICS members. TPAC committee member representatives from retailers Meijer, Target, JC Penney, Big Lots, Lord & Taylor, West Marine, Sears, Kohl's, and from GS1US were involved in course review and vetting before their public launch.

> NOTE: There is no endorsement, implied or explicit, by any person, association, corporation, or organization mentioned herein or not, with regards to my supplier education courses or to any of my other proposals or ideas.

This book is divided into several sections. The first section is my list of essential elements of supply chain vendor compliance. It is a checklist for customer/buyer enterprises which do not have a supply chain vendor compliance program in place. It is also a gap-analysis guide for customer/buyer enterprises that already have a vendor compliance program in place but are not achieving all of the desired goals. The development of a supply chain vendor compliance program is an introspective perspective into an enterprise's operations, technology, and policies with regards to its own capabilities and its viewpoint of its vendors. Because vendor compliance can be applied internally as well, a revealing self-examination may be performed with the mindset of how can the enterprise benefit from applying vendor compliance from within?

The second section of this book brings together key essential elements and presents how they function together under broader discussion topics such as legal framework, documentation, transactions, and performance monitoring. Where the essential elements list is objectively defined, the second section of the book will subjectively take several of the essential elements together and discuss how they combine to support or influence an enterprise's supply chain vendor compliance initiative.

The third part of this book is based on my supplier education courses and describes aspects of a vendor training regime that should be incorporated in a standard vendor compliance program. Understanding supply chain technology and terminology and how supply chain operations work is not the specialty of every vendor employee until their first foray into the world of vendor compliance, nor is it necessarily the expertise of customer enterprise employees either, so consider that this educational section provides valuable information for customer enterprise employees as well. As someone who is published and has gone through the editorial process I am well-acquainted with the need to write to one's audience, not assuming knowledge of the topic by the reader. Too often this fact is missed by those who write vendor compliance documentation for their enterprises. (This is one reason why I believed that industry-backed supplier education was a win-win situation.) Time is too often of the essence in vendor compliance, which is even more of a reason why supplier education makes sense. (Each of my six courses was not more than 60–90 minutes each in length.) Ensuring suppliers are educated as part of the vendor compliance process—preferably before but certainly during and on-going—is a critical component in keeping costs due to disruption down.

Customer enterprises have confessed to me that in establishing their own vendor compliance processes and documentation they either copied that of another company in their industry or from a company outside their industry: whosever specifications they were able to find on the Internet because they had no experience with vendor compliance themselves. This simply perpetuates and exasperates any bad behavior embedded in the source specifications and carried forward by inexperienced individuals. Frustrations flare for both the customer and the vendors and costs increase for all trading partners involved due to poor implementation of poorly understood and incorrectly sourced specifications.

Just because you can leverage size and strength does not mean you should. How an enterprise wields its might in terms of vendor compliance mandates is—from my experience—too often misdirected. With all the resources that some (multi-billion dollar) enterprises have I remain discouraged and disappointed that so little exertion, such juvenile effort, goes into supply chain vendor compliance. Lower costs, better prices, entrepreneurial opportunities that translate to economic lifts and less commoditization of the business model (depending upon the industry) are all within reach by simply doing a better job at supply chain vendor compliance. For all the enterprises that spout ethics it is time to translate those to understand that vendors are just as important as customers and employees and deserve better treatment than what they have been receiving, and there are plenty of rewards for everyone to reap from doing so.

The fourth part of the book begins with a short story that happened to one of my clients, a tale of a customer enterprise failing to see the proverbial forest through the trees and allowing their prospective vendors to take the practical—and ethical—pathway to success. Instead the result was a ridiculous waste of tens of thousands of dollars by my client and excessive lost hours on the part of the customer's buyer to get a single product set up, all to have the deal scuttled in the end by a disgruntled buyer and through no fault of the prospective vendor (my client). The backstory of ethical failures, insider deals, and shortsightedness makes the tale more egregious and exasperating.

Next is a section on the management of the data derived from a vendor compliance program and how this data drives information for supplier relationship management and supplier risk management programs. I examine the characteristics of vendor compliance data using five key aspects of Big Data. Since the formulas that rely on the data are topics that go hand-in-hand, I discuss the importance of getting the mathematics correct in a vendor compliance program, for both the customer and the vendor enterprise.

The fourth part of the book concludes by bringing together vendor compliance, supplier risk management, and good governance, appropriate given what happened to my client in the case study, as well as emphasizing the point that vendor compliance is equally a tactic for internal controls as it is a strategy for lower supply chain costs through uniformity in business operations through the interaction with the downstream supply chain. The concept of the customer and supplier is not just external to the enterprise but is applicable internally as well, and vendor compliance is at the core of both supplier relationship management and supplier risk management whereby the same supply chain data can be used to analyze supplier performance and supplier risk, as well as for supply chain fraud detection.

Preface

My first introduction to supply chain vendor compliance was in 1993 when I was the Information Technology Manager at a privately-owned apparel company that sold to national retailers in the United States. From there I moved on to be the Information Technology Manager at a medical products manufacturing and distribution company where supply chain vendor compliance was a top priority because the company sold to both national U.S. retailers and national medical product distributors.

Having been through several corporate restructurings, downsizings, and lay-offs (none of them my fault!) already in the first 11 years of my career since university graduation, and facing yet another (also not my fault!), fate may have been sending me a message that it was time to listen and I was strongly contemplating branching out on my own and becoming an independent consultant. I knew, however, that to thrive and not just survive I would need to specialize and be not just another commodity in the crowded field information technology. It was the result of an opportune lunch conversation with my barcode equipment vendor that made me realize my niche knowledge in the technical and operational aspects of supply chain vendor compliance that could very well be the differentiating factor in my consulting business model. On January 1, 1996 my company Katzscan Inc. (www.katzscan.com) was born and true to form supply chain vendor compliance has been a defining and differentiating niche specialty that I have combined with data analysis, automatic identification applications (e.g. barcode labeling and scanning such as fixed asset management, manufacturing work-in-process, inventory control, order picking-and-packing), operations improvement, Enterprise Resource Planning (ERP) software expertise, and fraud detection and prevention as my skills and business model has evolved.

My experience with Electronic Data Interchange (EDI) data structures, mapping, and EDI-ERP integration also dates to 1993 and my prior 11 years of software development and business analysis experience in sales order processing, invoicing and general accounting, inventory, point-of-sales, and manufacturing provided a solid foundation. My experience with barcode labeling and scanning applications (including software development and business analysis) started in 1991 and also proved very useful as EDI and barcode labeling are two critical technologies still relied upon in various supply chains such as retail, pharmaceuticals, electronics, and book publishing.

Supply chain vendor compliance encompasses both the technical and operational mandates that buying (customer) enterprises, primarily because they have the leverage to do so, impose upon their vendors, with the goal of bringing efficiencies to their operations. The technical aspects of supply chain vendor compliance primarily focus on electronic business-to-business (eB2B such as EDI) and auto-identification (e.g. barcode labeling and radio frequency identification), both as extensions of the ERP system. The operational aspects of vendor compliance encompass sales order processing, invoice processing, product picking and packing (a.k.a. distribution), shipment scheduling, distribution and shipping paperwork such as the pack list and bill of lading, carton pallet stacking, and carton and pallet label design and placement.

Just imagine a chain store retailer with several thousand vendors, (not unusual and likely a low number for a national U.S. retailer), but without vendor compliance guidelines which set uniform parameters for carton sizes, label specifications, shipping documentation, and shipment scheduling. It would be cost-prohibitive for the retailer to manage all of the variations that would abound from each vendor providing different-sized cartons (some of which may not fit on the retailer's conveyor belts at the distribution centers), labels without uniform data in human readable and barcode form for scanning, and packing lists and bills of lading without consistent item information. The retailer would not be able to collect all of the information necessary (e.g. if some vendors did not place barcode labels on their cartons) to manage its supply chain or the data collection effort itself would be in disarray from having to be customized for all vendor variations (e.g. the differences in what data each vendor put on their carton labels and what data the vendor also put in barcode form).

Vendor compliance guidelines are used by consumer product retail store chains and manufacturers, grocery stores and food manufacturers, automobile manufacturing, the United States federal government (including the military), pharmaceutical manufacturing and distribution, electronic component distribution, book publishing, and the marine industry. (This is not a complete list, just a sampling of industries from my experience.)

Where the Benefits Lie

Vendor compliance requirements are designed to remove the technical and operational variations between supply chain trading partners (a customer and a vendor) and create a single set of guidelines that vendors can follow. Truly the obvious beneficiary is the buying enterprise (the customer trading partner) that can impose the mandates upon the supplying enterprise (the vendor trading partner): most vendors bristle at having to implement costly technologies and operations processes for the luxury of being able to sell to their customers. Where customers achieve cost reductions vendors suffer cost increases to implement and keep up with the compliance mandates. Combined with being squeezed for more competitive prices it is little wonder that many vendors—in my experience—implement compliance requirements with resistance, doing what is needed to minimally get by and comply.

In truth, for vendors the implementation of compliance requirements is an opportunity for an introspective look at the enterprise's technology and operations; it is a chance for change and to use the upgrades to one's advantage. By receiving purchase orders electronically there is no longer the need for manual data entry, removing manual errors and time-intensive efforts. By barcode labeling items and cartons, barcode scanning can greatly minimize if not eliminate costly manual mistakes in the picking and packing process. But do not stop there: as long as items have barcodes why not switch inventory procedures to scan the item barcodes instead of manually counting? The opportunity to identify and barcode warehouse shelf locations also presents itself now.

Improving purchasing, manufacturing, raw materials and finished goods inventory procedures are all necessary now because running out of finished goods simply is not an option when a purchase order from a major customer comes in. And with probable short lead times given that many customers do not want to hold inventory longer than necessary, burdening their vendors with the cost instead, the vendor will have to improve its own supply chain management.

Not only will smart vendors take the opportunity to learn from their customers, but as I tell my clients who are vendors, it is a competitive advantage to be smarter than your customer and not just smarter your competitor. Some customers provide a wealth of product sales information back to their vendors that too often vendors do not take advantage of. Just because the customer is a big or very large enterprise does not or should not imply every one of their software systems are up-to-date and sophisticated. If a vendor can glean key information from the sales data provided by its customers, that data can be used to alter product attribute manufacturing and distribution decisions, "weaponize" (my term for making more intelligent and valuable) the vendor's sales representative during the next buyer meeting, and possibly open up new sales channel or marketing ideas.

Chargebacks: The Dissenter's Consequence

When vendors do not comply or err in compliance by mistake they are reprimanded by what is called a *chargeback*: a financial penalty for non-compliance deducted from an invoice payment. Sometimes the chargeback is taken from the invoice payment related to the deduction, e.g. the customer is paying the invoice related to the receipt of a shipment and several cartons had missing labels.

Other times chargebacks are applied weeks or months after the customer has received the goods. Depending on the information provided by the customer, the reconciling of the chargeback to the original order and subsequent shipment can be easy or difficult for the vendor. In these situations the deductions on the payment remittance have nothing in common with the invoice being paid because they reference unrelated orders on shipments farther passed.

Chargebacks have become so egregious in nature that vendors often believe they are simply a source of profit for the customer, a belief held especially true by vendors in the U.S. retail industry. As I discussed in my book *Detecting and Reducing Supply Chain Fraud* (Gower Publishing, August 2012) and will review later, chargebacks that exceed the cost of the correction may be illegal in the United States. This is a further irritation for vendors. But why then would customers go so far as to skirt laws for compliance: For profits or for other reasons?

True, some industries may run on narrow profits and very possibly use chargebacks as a profit-boost. But it is also true that even minor disruptions in supply chains can result in significant costs incurred and customer enterprises need vendors to perform exceptionally well, if not perfect. The problem is that customer enterprises do not return perfect performance in their judgment and treatment of their vendors, exasperating an imperfect relationship balance.

Customers need vendors to comply and thus ratchet up the penalty violations to make their point heard loud and clear: disruptions are costly and vendors need to follow the guidelines. Delays mean money and potentially lost sales if the delay results in an item not being available when a consumer wants to make a purchase. The customer of a vendor may be the vendor to another customer along the supply chain: performance pressures may unknowingly be rippling through the supply chain from one vendor to the next.

Being Your Own Worst Enemy

But throughout my experience, and for all the logical reasons there are for supply chain vendor compliance, what I found was that time and time again, the management of the vendor compliance programs by my employers' customers and by my clients' trading partners was, simply put and on the whole, substandard and far below my expectations especially when some of these trading partners (the customer enterprises) are multi-billion dollar entities who have the personnel and technical resources to do a much better job.

Documentation that failed to provide direction or conflicted with other documentation, poorly organized web sites, errors in eB2B mapping guidelines (on one occasion some that I caught for the retailer during testing), eB2B mapping requirements that contradict the standards, lack of label template examples and barcode specifications, under-staffing of vendor resources, inability to communicate to vendor compliance resources by any other means than a web portal, lack of specific vendor contacts, compliance guidelines with unintended consequences, and differing customer enterprise opinions on how to interpret the same vendor compliance instruction depending upon which person the vendor communicated with, are all the symptoms of poorly implemented and managed vendor compliance programs that result in increased costs for both the customer and the vendor. The more the customer enterprise has to engage with the vendor the more the operational costs increase: it is such a simple formula. But flat-out refusing to communicate to vendors is not an acceptable solution!

Excessive costs are borne in the distribution center, in information technology, and in the office staff. Frustrations are felt by both the customer and the vendor. Any delays that result in getting the product from the vendor to the customer may result in a lost consumer sale. Penalizing vendors with chargebacks for poorly implemented compliance requirements is more than just a slap in the face, it becomes downright unethical.

What I find sadly laughable is that the same customer-buyer enterprises that talk of supply chain efficiencies and in some instances are awarded for their supply chain prowess are the guiltiest of parties when it comes to their vendor compliance programs from my experience. For all the talk of driving efficiencies into the supply chain, cutting costs, shortening lead times, and better customer-vendor relationships, I have seen scant evidence of improvements in any vendor compliance programs towards these goals.

And yet of all the endeavors available to do better, improving vendor compliance program management is in my opinion the most achievable and would benefit both the customer and the vendor. The purpose of this book is to outline the elements that comprise a quality vendor compliance program and discuss the correct way of effectively implementing them. In doing so and following these guidelines an enterprise will cut costs and reduce risks associated with its vendor compliance program. The results are smoother-running supply chains, better supplier relationships, and lower operating costs.

Introduction

Whom do enterprises value more: their customers or their vendors?

From public government entities to private corporations, enterprises speak extensively about their commitment to their suppliers especially when it comes to supplier diversity. In the United States "supplier diversity" typically refers to the extension of business to firms owned by minorities or selected groups such as African-American, Hispanic, women, or military veterans. Supplier diversity is a law and is a sign of good corporate citizenship.

But based on the way some enterprises – especially in the private sector – seem to treat their vendors, my bet on the answer to the question I asked is on "customers". I have experienced this from my own clients who believe that they have some kind of right to mistreat their vendors because their customers mistreat them as a vendor. The perpetuation of all this mistreatment must at some point stop!

In something akin to a positive feedback mechanism, (but substituting negative energy for positive feedback), what large enterprises fail to realize is that their business models suffer due to their poorly managed vendor compliance programs. It is not just in the excessive costs that they are inflicting on their vendors, but also by causing themselves to endure excessive operating costs in the mismanagement of the vendor compliance program. These costs run through the customer-buyer enterprise from the distribution facility, information technology, vendor relations, and accounting. All of these costs take their toll, either being passed along to the consumer as higher product prices or preventing an enterprise from investing in additional employees or software projects due to higher costs of goods sold (lower profit margin).

The customer-buyer enterprise may also be hurting its competitive ability by becoming more of a commodity business through the exclusion of vendors because of overly complicated vendor compliance processes and guidelines that effectively disqualify vendors at the product presentation stage. When seeking to differentiate from one's competitor price and product selection are two key factors that consistently pop up in advertisements. In retail if competitor store chains offer the same or very similar goods consumers may be more likely to view them as a commodity rather than one that has unique goods that is more likely to draw in shoppers. Commodity competitors are forced to compete on price where margins are lower and customer loyalty is fickle.

In some supply chains such as retail and grocery some enterprises may have a strong desire to allow local managers to purchase from local suppliers. Unfortunately the local managers might find their own enterprise vendor compliance programs prevent the business relationship with local suppliers from being established because the same complex vendor compliance rules and requirements are being applied to local suppliers as to national fulfilment vendors.

Vendor compliance is important for supply chain efficiencies, and vendors understand this when it is explained to them. But the poor implementation and mismanagement of a vendor compliance program will only result in increased costs for both the customer enterprise and vendor community, driving a wedge in between the trading partner relationship. Assessing vendors financial penalties for non-compliance will only exasperate the problem especially if the customer enterprise is unable to accurately perform problem root-cause analysis and sets penalty fees in excess of the actual cost of the correction.

Well run vendor compliance programs should help vendors self-implement and control costs, not force vendors to rely on constant communication and increase costs for all trading partners involved. The purpose of this book is to expose the weaknesses in traditional vendor compliance programs and to identify the characteristics of well-managed vendor compliance programs that foster beneficial trading partner relationships. A well-executed vendor compliance program can control and decrease costs by reducing disruptions throughout the supply chain, from the distribution center to the data center to the corporate office. Competition is fierce, and the right vendor can help define a business model, react quickly to changes, and differentiate between you and your competitors. Vendor compliance data sits at the core of supplier relationship management and supplier risk management, and the data can also be used for the detection and reduction of supply chain fraud.

'Because great partnerships—like great relationships—really are important.' Norman Katz

PART I

The Essential Elements

Introduction

The Essential Elements of Effective Supply Chain Vendor Compliance is designed to be a comprehensive list of topics to review when considering the implementation of a supply chain vendor compliance program, or if seeking to determine where an existing vendor compliance program is floundering due to gaps or weaknesses in certain key areas. The implementation of a vendor compliance program must happen in phases, and begins with a thoughtful examination of the customer enterprise itself: what are the technical and operational capabilities that the enterprise has at its ready? What are the challenges, e.g. technical and operational constraints, which exert limits that prevent the enterprise from achieving its vendor compliance goals? What are the resource constraints (e.g. budget money, expertise) that may confine or force to redefine the scope of the project?

Not all enterprises that sell are cut out to become supply chain vendors due to a lack of resources or a lack of commitment to the cause. Similarly, not all enterprises that buy are able to institute supply chain vendor compliance programs. In both cases there must be conscious thought given to what it means to implement vendor compliance. In this part of the book I will examine the fundamental components for buying enterprises that want to implement vendor compliance programs and drive efficiencies in their down-stream supply chain.

Envision

In defining a vendor compliance program it is necessary to understand what it is supposed to do and why it is being done. In my opinion, the purpose of vendor compliance is to create a uniform set of written business rules of engagement between the customer ("buyer") enterprise and the vendor ("seller") enterprises with whom the customer is involved in a trading partnership. Vendor compliance brings efficiency to the customer's business operations by creating a uniform set of guidelines that all vendors follow when conducting business with the customer. With all vendors operating under the same set of rules, the customer enterprise can operate more efficiently. For example if all of a customer enterprise's vendors used a different barcode label format on the exterior of the shipping cartons the customer would have to manage all the different variations of barcodes and data by vendor, a task financially unachievable and operationally unattainable given that some of the data is likely vendor-specific or only vendor identifiable. The customer's systems would have to be tailored to the myriad of variations in the data by vendor, which could be subject to change without notice. In contrast, the customer should follow industry standards in setting vendor compliance rules so that vendors can limit the variations in customer data and operational requirements. (Vendors deserve the same consideration in maintaining as much consistency in their systems and operations as possible when dealing with different customers.)

The vendor compliance documentation should be considered the code of conduct between the customer and the vendor. Should any disputes arise between the customer and the vendor, especially those that are settled through legal actions, the vendor compliance documentation will likely prevail in establishing the constructs and confines of the customer-vendor relationship.

> Supply Chain Vendor Compliance: *The requirements, as mandated by the buyer and agreed upon by the seller, that govern the trading partner relationship in the buyer's acquisition of goods and services from the seller.*

The following are questions that should be asked and analysis that should be investigated before a customer enterprise considers beginning a vendor compliance program.

1. What are the goals of the vendor compliance program?

2. Who is on the vendor compliance team? Who is the leader?

3. What process or technology gaps need to be closed?

4. What is the vendor viewpoint?

5. What percent of the supply chain is governable?

Sample goals are to increase accuracy, increase throughput, reduce paperwork ("go green"), increase controls and monitoring (for supplier risk analysis and for vendor performance analysis), and reduce exceptions to standard operating procedures. These goals can be achieved via the use of key supply chain technologies (Enterprise Resource Planning (ERP) system, Electronic Business-To-Business (eB2B) transactions, and Electronic Data Capture (EDC), each of which will be reviewed later) and the implementation of supply chain best practices (Examine, Evaluate, Enforce albeit with Empathy, Ethics, and Equality, each of which will be reviewed later.)

Vendor compliance is a team approach involving the functional areas of accounting, distribution (warehouse), buying (which is a different function than purchasing), logistics, product development, purchasing, sales, marketing, technology, and vendor relations. The team should be led by someone with knowledge of these functional areas, how they interact technically, and how they collaborate operationally towards the goals of the enterprise. This person should be empowered by executive management to affect the changes necessary to maintain the right balance between what the vendors are required to do and what the customer (the buying enterprise) needs the vendors to do.

> The gap between vendor requirements and customer necessities is one that demands investigation and examination as to the best place for resolution: vendor requirement or customer project? Pushing problems—inadequacies if you will—onto the backs of the vendor community because the customer enterprise does not want to invest in fixing a problem is the wrong direction for the customer enterprise to take. Require vendors to do only what is reasonable for them to do and what should—or only could—be performed by the vendor technically and operationally. What responsibilities can and should be performed by the customer enterprise should be done so.

As vendor compliance guidelines are developed there must be a team review to ensure that no one functional area's requirement conflicts with the needs of another functional area, and that the whole of the compliance requirement makes sense. There are few things more frustrating to a vendor than to have different customer vendor representatives provide different answers or interpretations to the same question with regard to a vendor compliance requirement or to have different compliance requirements in conflict and try to get different vendor representatives from the customer enterprise together to resolve them. These are not burdens the vendor should have to tolerate.

If the customer enterprise does not have certain technologies in place that are required to meet its vision those technologies should be successfully implemented before a vendor compliance program is rolled out. New technology that affects business operations such as eB2B and EDC often will require changes to existing business processes. Get those missing technologies in place and working, then roll them out to your vendor community in stages, and then phase them in to the other aspects of the vendor compliance program such as performance monitoring and chargebacks (both of which will be discussed later).

Are the vendors viewed as collaborators or combatants? If you consider your vendors as entities that you believe you can whip at your whim your vendor compliance program will likely be a costly and hard fought battle. You may lose some vendors by implementing a program that has unrealistic requirements. If you understand that your vendors are truly collaborative trading partners and have as much value to the enterprise as your employees and customers you will more likely find that your vendor compliance program implementation goes a lot smoother. In fact by engaging some of your vendors as part of the vendor compliance development process you might receive some insights and ideas on how to improve aspects of your vendor compliance program before it goes live as well as on betterments via a continuous monitoring cycle.

With this in mind it is important to understand what percent of your supply chain is governable. (Semantics aside, implementing vendor compliance does require the customer enterprise to be able to administer over the vendors: what I am trying to impress here is that there is a right way and a wrong way to govern.) This is important because this analysis helps to align vendor compliance program initiatives with desired goals and realities. There are different ways to perform this analysis.

One perspective is to tally all of the vendors and determine the percentage of vendors that the enterprise is able to leverage. If the percentage is too low then the customer enterprise may not reap full benefit in its vendor compliance initiative. For example, if a customer enterprise has 100 vendors but can leverage over only 65 percent this may warrant a re-examination of some of the vendor compliance program initiatives and goals.

Another—and probably more accurate—measure is to examine the percent of product purchased from vendors. If the enterprise has 100 vendors and believes it has leverage over 90 percent of the vendors that would seem to support a vendor compliance program. But if one of the 10 percent of the vendors it does not have leverage over provides 40 percent of its goods the enterprise may want to re-examine the overall impact of a vendor compliance program again, because the percentage amount of overall compliance will be low based on the total amount of goods that flow through the supply chain.

In almost all instances the customer enterprise is still able to reap benefits from the implementation of a vendor compliance program by some margin, and the extent of the benefits will vary based on the percent of vendors/ products the customer is able to influence to conform to the vendor compliance requirements. The return-on-investment of some aspects of the vendor compliance program may be longer-term than anticipated.

Explain

Your vendor compliance documentation will be written for two audiences: one internal and one external, and there should be no assumption that either audience is knowledgeable about the subject matter. People change jobs that result in knowledge departing with them, employees take on new roles too often without the benefit of enough training, and new hires direct from university will require more in-depth detail than experienced career employees. All this holds true for employees of customers and vendors alike, so it is beneficial when writing vendor compliance documentation to consider the need for clarity for both the internal and external audiences.

Like documentation prepared for Sarbanes-Oxley compliance or ISO (International Organization for Standardization) certification, vendor compliance guidelines ultimately describe how an enterprise operates and should therefore be prepared with an exacting level of detail. No assumption of knowledge should be presumed on the part of the author. Industry buzzwords and terminology should be clearly defined first, and customer-specific acronyms should be kept to a minimum to avoid both confusion with industry-specific terms and eroding the overall clarity of the documentation itself. "Distribution Center," "Fulfillment Center," "Warehouse," "Distribution Facility," and "Store Support Center" are all terms I have seen used by customers to describe the buildings where goods are received from vendors for distribution. Cleverness just causes confusion: keep the terminology familiar. Worse, I have witnessed customer's vendor compliance documentation—manuals, web sites, presentations, and e-mails—get lazy and then just refer to these buildings by abbreviation (DC, DF, FC, SSC) with no reference forcing the vendor to leap to the definition, if at all possible, based on the context. Stop reinventing new terminology for the same recognizable thing. Spell the terms out all the time to remove any confusion and complexity for the reader: it takes so little effort and adds so much value.

Key vendor compliance information includes the following list, which will be reviewed later in the book:

-     Vendor compliance guidelines

- Routing information

- Product preparation guidelines

- Item, carton, and pallet label and tag specifications

- eB2B mapping guidelines

- eB2B technical information

- Contact lists

- Chargeback guide

Exceptions

Every enterprise has them: they are the opposite of the standard operating procedures. Exceptions are typically the time-wasters and the cost-contributors. As destructive as they can be for an enterprise to manage, imagine trying to get external entities like vendors to understand, let alone build in to their software applications and standard operating procedures, especially when the exceptions are not their own.

> This is not to say that variations to procedures do not occur and should not occur under the course of daily business, e.g. small packages weighing less than 150 pounds use one carrier and those weighing 150 pounds or more use another carrier. These different situations exist in business operations and are readily covered by clearly defining the rules for which, in this example, one package carrier should be chosen versus another. This example is not as much an exception as it is a typical business rule for package delivery in the United States and is a uniform business rule applicable to small package delivery, beyond the rules or requirements of the customer enterprise.

It is where the exceptions are undefined or the rules convoluted or so complicated or contrary to industry norms that the exception becomes what should be too great a burden to pass to the vendor; the customer enterprise must alleviate these complex exceptions before they become part of the vendor compliance requirements. If the exception is customer-specific it must be resolved and removed before being passed on to the vendor community. The excuse that the customer enterprise does not want to put the resources into its remediation is a false one. The failure by the customer enterprise to deal with an exception will only result in higher costs incurred in the execution of the vendor compliance program through greater operational and organizational disruptions as the exception is continually questioned by the vendor community as to how to work around the issue and internally by the customer enterprise's own staff as it is dealt with separately through different business processes and technical workarounds. Costs borne by the vendor community, and this includes the costs of vendor compliance, are ultimately passed along to the customer in higher prices. It is the customer enterprise that can maintain control over this vicious cycle by removing exceptions, which increase vendor costs.

In U.S. retail it is typical for large items, e.g. mattresses and furniture, to be shipped to specific distribution centers equipped to handle them; likewise sometimes jewelry and very expensive electronics are directed to certain distribution centers equipped with secure holding areas. These exceptions are clear-cut and relatively easy for a vendor to follow. If the exception cannot be easily defined and documented for the vendor then the customer enterprise must rethink why the exception exists and either do away with the exception or redefine it in a much simpler set of parameters for vendors to follow. This is true of both operational and technical exceptions.

Expectations

The customer enterprise should define what expectations it has for itself and for its vendor community and whether those expectations are in sync with each other. Can all vendors meet the enterprise's purchase order requirements in terms of order quantities and timeframes? Are the vendors able to turnaround eB2B document transactions in the timeframe required by the customer enterprise? Is the customer enterprise itself able to be absolute in its determination of compliance violations before it acts as judge, jury, and executioner and withholds money for financial penalties? It is fine to set the proverbial bar relatively, albeit realistically, high in the beginning as the concept of the vendor compliance initiative is envisioned, but as the truth of what the customer enterprise and vendor community is each capable of there needs to be a reality-check that expectations do not exceed capabilities for all participants involved.

Implementing a vendor compliance program is a work-in-progress. The customer enterprise should allow sufficient time for vendors to get acquainted with and up-to-speed on the new requirements as they are implemented in phases. The customer enterprise should set the initial expectation low—or certainly reasonable—until bugs, problems, and snafus are all worked out. Vendor feedback will be critical and will help identify missed issues where the customer enterprise overlooked or underestimated aspects of the implementation.

The customer enterprise should realize this is a collaborative opportunity and by engaging with select vendors can work through its own kinks in getting its operational changes smoothed out and the flaws in its new technology worked through. As a consultant I have worked with several vendor clients as they have helped their trading partner customers at the beginning of their foray into vendor compliance. It is an opportunity for the vendor to have their voice heard in how some aspects of the customer's vendor compliance guidelines are being refined: what works well and what does not. It also forges a stronger relationship between the vendor willing to take the time and added expense to help their customer.

Enroll

The process of vendor enrollment in its information gathering can perform seller qualification and some baseline risk assessment as well. It is—by definition—the process where information about a prospective vendor should be recorded and reviewed for determination as to whether the seller company qualifies as a vendor.

A basic vendor profile should inquire as to the overall structure of the selling company, asking pertinent questions such as:

- What month and year was the business started? Where was the business established? How long has the business existed at its current location?

- Who are the business owners? Backgrounds of the business owners may be important, so address and nationality information of the owners may be a requirement.

- What is the business classification? (In the U.S. business classification types include: sole proprietorship, C corporation, S corporation, Partnership, and Limited Liability Company.)

- Insurance coverage types and claims limits.

- Addresses and types (e.g. office, company-owned distribution center, third party logistics provider, manufacturing center) of locations.

- Number of employees.

- E-business capabilities (e.g. is the company currently capable of conducting business electronically?).

- Contact information for: technology, accounting, shipping and logistics, product information, product orders, vendor compliance.

- GS1 identifier (for companies selling consumer or pharmaceutical products—more on this later in the book).

Asking prospective vendors for financial information such as a letter from a manager from the company's financial institution stating the length of time the prospective vendor has had their account active can be helpful in assessing risk. (However a change in financial institutions by no means is a risk indicator by itself as it is not an uncommon occurrence.) Requesting reference sources from other customers of the prospective vendor provides insight into who the company is selling to now, if at all, and whether your company is likely to be the prospective vendor's first customer or the first similar customer in terms of size or industry sector.

In the United States, diversity in vendor selection is a priority and even a requirement at the government level. Asking if the prospective vendor is a minority-owned (e.g. women, Hispanic, African-American, military veteran) business may be important. Also in the United States, the Census Bureau of the federal government maintains the North American Industry Classification System (NAICS), which can be found at https://www.census.gov/eos/www/naics/. Classifying vendors by the six-digit NAICS codes provides a means of grouping them by the same standard used by the U.S. government for analyzing vendors (e.g. purchasing, performance, percentage of total) by specific type. For example, all codes that begin with 44 and 45 belong to the Retail Trade category. Within Retail Trade category 44 all codes beginning with 442 belong to the Furniture and Home Furnishing Stores group. The six-digit NAICS code is an intelligent hierarchical numbering system. NAICS categories 31–33 cover Manufacturing; within category 31 codes prefixed with 313, 314, and 315 representing textile, fabric, and apparel products and codes prefixed with 316 represent footwear products.

Key product attribute questions should include the following:

- Country of origin / manufacture

- Product dimensions and weight

- Product consumer attributes (e.g. styles, colors, and sizes)

- Product description

- Vendor product code and Global Trade Item Number (GTIN)

- Product cost (the vendor's product price)

- Hazardous materials and material safety data sheets

- Product packaging (how many units per carton, carton size and weight, how many cartons per pallet)

- Lead time (likely measured in days or weeks)

- Constraints (e.g. maximum number of units per month)

- Minimum order quantity

- Maximum order quantity (per order and per month)

- Order quantity multiples (e.g. if the order quantity multiple was 12, orders for 12, 24, 36, and 48 would be acceptable, but an order for a quantity of 40 would be rejected by the vendor)

These questions help the buying enterprise paint the picture of its relationship with the prospective vendor, at least at the beginning, by understanding expectations based on what the prospective vendor has stated they are capable of doing especially in terms of the maximum number of units per month and the manufacturing lead time. The customer has the option, based on knowing the prospective vendor's limitations, of accepting or rejecting entering into a trading partner relationship with the company. The prospective vendor may become guilty of overpromising but with the answers recorded it is strictly the vendor who would have failed in living up to the terms of the relationship.

Any alterations necessary—such as carton sizes or units per carton—should be made during the enrollment process.

Educate

After a selling company becomes enrolled as a vendor, the next step is to ensure that trading partner is educated as to the requirements necessary for a successful relationship. Having well-written vendor compliance documentation does not alleviate the necessity for vendor education.

The education process serves useful purposes:

1. It enables understanding gaps to be closed. Even with well-written vendor compliance documentation some vendors may struggle in their understanding of industry verbiage or technical terminology.

2. It provides feedback on the vendor compliance documentation itself and enables the customer enterprise to revise the documentation based on the reaction from the vendor community.

3. It delivers an introspective critique at the customer enterprise's operations with the chance to improve processes as they relate to vendor interactions. Vendors may provide valuable insights into gaps or better ways that the customer enterprise was unaware of.

4. It fosters the greater collaborative relationship between the customer and vendor, highlighting the customer's policy of "educate" instead of "dictate." Such a vendor-friendly environment may lead to vendors approaching the customer enterprise with cost-saving ideas, offering to partner on larger supply chain projects, introducing new products to the customer enterprise as opposed to a competitor, or partnering on testing new customer supply chain initiatives.

Vendor education medium can take the form of documentation, presentation, webinars, or videos. Documentation would likely be the least effective form because the vendor compliance requirements are already documented: education should be more interactive. Gathering vendors for live presentations is an expensive proposition, especially for small vendors to afford, and does not allow for a regular schedule to occur. Webinars, whether live or recorded, are likely the most practical approach and the best use of available technology. The webinar can utilize presentation materials with clear graphical images that highlight concepts. Live webinars offer question submission capability so vendor audience viewers can submit inquiries for answer either during the webinar, at the end of the webinar, or distributed to attendees shortly after the end of the webinar. These individual webinar questions provide the customer enterprise an analytical opportunity to develop a frequently asked questions section on their vendor compliance web site until the vendor compliance documentation is improved. The more information that is available to vendors without the need to involve people at the customer enterprise, the lower the cost of administering the vendor compliance program.

Education should go beyond just the compliance documentation and showcase some of the inner workings (technology and operations) of the customer enterprise in either video or graphics form. Some suggestions are:

- How the barcode or radio frequency identification tag on a carton is used to verify the receipt against an electronic business-to-business document such as the shipment notification.

- The inventory situations that trigger a purchase order to be created and sent to vendors electronically.

- How an invoice is received, matched to the purchase order, matched to the shipment receipt, and paid to the vendor.

- How all the electronic document transactions (e.g. purchase order, purchase order acknowledgement, purchase order change, invoice, payment remittance, credit/debit adjustment, advance ship notice, functional acknowledgement) work together.

- Examples of common financial penalties for compliance infractions and how they can be minimized.

Certainly the issue with education is that it takes time and money to put together and execute but the return-on-investment is, in my opinion, well worth the expenditure because of the benefits of reduced operational overhead with a more informed vendor community. Sending vendors to industry standard web sites like GS1 is not education, it is a knowledge reference, yet too often this is what is substituted for education by too many customer enterprises. The third part of this book is dedicated to the education initiative.

Enterprise Resource Planning

The Enterprise Resource Planning (ERP) software system sits at the very center of the suite of core supply chain technologies—along with Electronic Business-To-Business (eB2B) and Electronic Data Capture (EDC)—that are essential for an effective vendor compliance program. The ERP system is very simply the system of record for: the entities (customers and vendors) an enterprise transacts business with; the items (raw materials, components, and finished goods) that are the subject of the transactions; the transactions themselves (purchase orders, sales orders, manufacturing work orders, and invoices); where, how many, and the value of its inventory of items; and to account for everything (payables, receivables, general ledger). The ERP system tends to define how an enterprise operates because every movement along the supply chain is performed via a feature of the ERP system where it is recorded and tracked. eB2B and EDC—both which will be discussed next—are extensions of the ERP system: eB2B an external extension and EDC an internal extension.

Electronic Business-To-Business

Consider the basic business transactions, e.g. purchase orders, invoices, and shipping notices, which are conducted between a customer enterprise and its vendors. Now add some common confirmation transactions: when a purchase order is sent by the customer the items, quantities, and prices are to be acknowledged by the vendor; when the vendor sends an invoice (a request for payment) and the customer submits a payment, the customer should also send a document indicating what transactions (what purchase orders or invoices) are being paid. If there are any credits or debits that affect the payment, a separate credit/debit adjustment transaction should be sent to the vendor in addition. When the vendor sends a shipment a document outlining the physical characteristics of the shipment and detailing the contents is sent to the shipment recipient, the customer enterprise. Place on top of all that a very congenial protocol that states that every business document sent will be at minimum acknowledged as to having been received or not. (The receipt of the acknowledgment is the confirmation that the document sent was received; the lack of an acknowledgment after 24 business hours is a strong indication that the sent document was never received.)

Certainly all of those transactions could be performed via telephone, facsimile, postal mail, and e-mail. The primary problem is that doing so requires a significant amount of manual effort in customer and vendor communication through these methods. Each communication method has its inherent weaknesses when it comes to information delivery and receipt. And managing the individual transactions manually also results in manually reconciling the transactions: e.g. purchase order and purchase order acknowledgment, purchase order and invoice, invoice and payment remittance, invoice or payment remittance and debit/credit adjustment. The ship notice is often reconciled with the barcode carton or pallet label scans, or radio frequency tag reads, when the shipment arrives at the warehouse.

Telephone communications are not memorialized (written down) as a document of record. Manual transcription errors can occur and are subjective in nature. Most people would likely object to having their conversations recorded, and then there is the problem of storing the recording and the ability to keyword search them for specific conversation retrieval. It is inefficient for use for comprehensive transactions such as purchase orders of many line items, especially as it binds a person to the task for an extended period of time.

Facsimile communications are subject to machine errors (e.g. paper jams, print quality problems) and simply getting lost or misdirected on the receiving end. Facsimile confirmations are only a confirmation that the receiving machine received the data transmission; they are not a confirmation of acceptance of delivery terms, quantity, and price as in the case of the purchase order acknowledgment. For some facsimile machines the receipt and the printed output may be two distinctly separate actions where the success of the first (the receipt) has nothing to do with the failure of the latter (the printed output). Facsimile machines had their time and were great for the functionality and efficiency they provided but the speed and volume of today's business demands more.

Postal mail—at least regular mail without any receipt confirmation—is just too slow to meet the rapid demands of business today in most supply chains across all document transactions possibly with the exception of payments, even though paperwork reduction initiatives at many enterprises are transitioning from traditional checks to bank-to-bank transfers. The expense of receipt-verified mail through either the postal delivery service or that of third-party services becomes prohibitively expensive rather quickly considering even the modest quantity of business documents transacted by small companies, let alone the massive scale of documents generated by large enterprises and their supply chain trading partners.

(Neither facsimile nor postal mail solves the problem of having the data manually entered into the ERP system, a time-consuming, error-prone, and expensive proposition. Businesses have been expressly seeking to move away from—not towards—paper-based methodologies.)

E-mail is simply the faster replacement of postal mail. Even with the read-receipt option (which not all e-mail systems generate) as a means of verifying that a message was read, e-mail communications, especially those with attachments, are mostly manual by nature. While automated outbound e-mail communications can solve the manual intervention problem on the customer end, ensuring the e-mail passes through each vendor's spam filter, anti-virus, and firewall settings, keeping vendor e-mail addresses up-to-date, and not being rejected by full vendor e-mail boxes are issues and constraints that the customer enterprise will have to handle in choosing this communication methodology. Extracting data from formatted inbound e-mail attachments such as spreadsheets is a step in the right direction. However, formatted spreadsheets will require manual entry by vendors and thus may be an undue burden and subject to data entry errors (e.g. data inconsistencies from an originating transaction), beyond those which can be corralled through standard spreadsheet data field edit controls.

Simply acquiring an Enterprise Resource Planning (ERP) system or similar business software application that has within its capabilities purchase order generation and invoice payment is not enough: what is needed is to automate—at minimum—the delivery, receipt, and confirmation of business documents as electronic transactions. With the basic business documents in electronic format residing in the ERP system, reconciling them to their complimentary counterparts would be a logical next step, but first things first.

In the United States the method of eB2B between companies that is most widely used is called Electronic Data Interchange (EDI), the standards which are maintained by the Accredited Standards Committee (ASC X12, www.x12. org) as chartered by the American National Standards Institute (www.ansi. org). For the rest of the world the United Nations Electronic Data Interchange For Administration, Commerce and Transport (UN/EDIFACT) standard is more commonly used. While I would normally find a Wikipedia page suspect in content, the following information that I have summarized here taken from http://en.wikipedia.org/wiki/X12_EDIFACT_Mapping overall seems to accurately denote the common EDI business documents and highlights the similar corresponding EDIFACT transaction. Note that all EDI documents are known by name, abbreviation, and a unique numerical identifier the latter of which is shown in the cross-reference table (Table 1.1).

Table 1.1   EDI-EDIFACT EB2B Transaction Sets

TRANSACTION SET/DOCUMENT	ANSI (EDI)	EDIFACT
PRODUCT/PRICING TRANSACTIONS		
Price Sales Catalog	832	PRICAT
Price Authorization Acknowledgement/Status	845	ATHSTS
Specification/Technical Information	841	PRDSPE
Request For Quotation	840	REQOTE
Response To Request For Quotation	843	QUOTES
ORDERING TRANSACTIONS		
Purchase Order	850	ORDERS
Purchase Order Acknowledgement	855	ORDRSP
Purchase Order Change	860	ORDCHG
Purchase Order Change Acknowledgement	865	ORDRSP
Order Status Inquiry	869	ORSSTA
Order Status Report	870	ORDREP
Product Activity Data	852	SLSRPT
MATERIALS MANAGEMENT TRANSACTIONS		
Planning Schedule/Material Release	830	DELFOR
Shipping Schedule	862	DELJIT
Ship Notice/manifest (ASN)	856	DESADV
Report of Test Results	863	QALITY
SHIPPING/RECEIVING TRANSACTIONS		
Shipment Information (Bill of Lading)	858	IFTMCS
Receiving Advice	861	RECADV
Non-conformance Information-Disposition Transaction, Cause/Correction	842	NONCON
INVENTORY MANAGEMENT TRANSACTIONS		
Inventory Inquiry/Advice	846	INVRPT
Product Transfer Account Adjustment	844	SSDCLM
FINANCIAL TRANSACTIONS		
Invoice	810	INVOIC
Freight Invoice	859	IFTMCS
Payment order/Remittance Advice (EFT)	820	REMADV
CONTROL TRANSACTIONS		
Functional Acknowledgement	997	CONTRL
Application Advice	824	APERAK
Trading Partner Profile	838	PARTIN

The benefits of interfacing the ERP system with eB2B result in:

- A single instance of data entry or data export for each transaction.

- No wasted effort for document transmission to the vendor, e.g. there is no printing, no need for the employee to leave their desk to retrieve the printout, no trips to the facsimile machine, and no long-distance facsimile communications. Further, the employee is not otherwise engaged, sometimes socially, during trips to and from the printer and facsimile machine.

- No non-value-added efforts by employees in follow-up to ensure e-mails, postal mail, and facsimiles have been received and the management of what documents by identifier (e.g. purchase orders by purchase order number) have been sent to which vendor and by what communication methodology.

Getting small vendors on-board with eB2B solutions was previously a very difficult proposition, and one that sometimes required very large enterprises to solve by the creation of their own vendor eB2B portals. Sometimes vendors had little choice but to invest in eB2B communication and translation software for thousands of dollars (U.S.). For the majority of small vendors these eB2B software applications were disconnected from the myriad of small business software systems they used to manage their businesses; this made their eB2B software investment—which could range from $2500US to $5000US initially before the costs per trading partner specifications were included—the equivalent of a fancy facsimile machine in that inbound transactions (such as purchase orders) were printed for data entry into their business software system, and outbound transactions (such as invoices) were manually data entered into the eB2B software for outbound transmission after they were printed from the business software application.

The growth of Internet-based applications—and as web-based technology has evolved—has shifted the landscape of solutions from software-based to service-based even for many large customer enterprises who have decided to outsource the translation and distribution of documents to their vendors and the receipt and translation of inbound documents from their vendors. Web-based solution pricing is typically more affordable than software pricing and very achievable for even the smallest of vendors: staring costs can be similar to a robust smartphone cellular plan on a monthly basis, and there is no costly initial investment or traditional software maintenance fees.

With no software required the vendor accesses a web-based portal from their computer, (any computer connected to the Internet), to receive purchase orders, send ship notifications, print carton and pallet labels, and send invoices. Some of these transactions are generated based on each other: for example the ship notice is based on what items are selected from the purchase order; the invoice is based on what items were transmitted in the ship notice. Most web-based portals allow for data to be downloaded in common file format (e.g. spreadsheet compatible or text file) for mapping to a business software application (e.g. ERP system), and some web-based portal providers already have developed application program interfaces to common business software applications and ERP systems for data integration purposes. Web-based portal applications have removed the cost-prohibitive barrier to supply chain enablement: eB2B is no longer unachievable but is now something available to all trading partners within the supply chain regardless of their global location and company size.

The extension of the ERP system via eB2B enables a customer enterprise to more efficiently and more effectively communicate and transact with its vendor trading partners. The effectiveness of the eB2B communications is in its protocol whereby the receipt of a transaction is acknowledged in kind. It is this effectiveness that leads to the efficiency of less manual follow-up due to the unknowns of whether a business document was received, and instead allows automated management by exception reporting highlighting only in cases where delayed vendor trading partner responses should be investigated. Optionally the receiving trading partner may pass the document through business logic and report back to the sender with regards to the structure and content of the document that was received, identifying file integrity errors and business logic errors as part of the automated process. File integrity errors may be diversions from the agreed-upon data file layouts and could be caused by software flaws or mis-scheduled upgrades. Business logic errors could include anything ranging from sending a vendor a purchase order for an item that is not theirs, pricing mismatches, incorrect quantities (e.g. if an item must be purchased in quantity multiples of 12 but an order for 15 is submitted) that could be due to software issues or data setup errors. For both trading partners the ability to use automation to catch errors and reduce data entry (which can produce its own set of errors) is more effective—and brings more efficiency—than other methods of transacting business especially when the quantity of the transactions scales for one or both of the trading partners is beyond the ability to conduct business via any other means.

Electronic Data Capture

Another way to extend the reach of the Enterprise Resource Planning system is to implement Electronic Data Capture (EDC) by scanning (such as via traditional laser) or imaging (performed akin to using digital camera technology enabling one or many symbols to be captured and analyzed in a single snapshot) barcodes or reading radio-frequency identification (RFID) tags. Identification can be done at any of the item, carton, and pallet levels. EDC should be used as part of the process when goods are received against a purchase order and can also be used for inventory movement (e.g. raw materials to manufacturing), order fulfillment (picking of goods for customer orders), and physical inventory counting.

Much like eB2B, EDC offers the benefits of effectiveness (in terms of higher rates of accuracy) and efficiency (faster throughput) in operations processes. This is important for both the trading partner relationship (in terms of assessing vendor performance) and the buying enterprise's ability to ultimately move goods through its supply chain, whether it is cross-dock or across facilities, to meet its own customers' demand schedules.

For customer enterprises a key issue is what standards should apply when deciding on the format of the item, carton, or pallet barcode label? The global standards organization, GS1 (www.gs1.org) has a General Specifications guideline document in their Standards knowledge center that—at 478 pages for their 2014 version—is packed with information about barcode standards and usages as well as sample templates for item, carton, and pallet labels. Different barcode symbologies (languages) have specific uses within the supply chain. Global Trade Identification Numbers (GTINs) now adorn items where there were once Universal Product Codes (UPCs) in the United States and European Article Numbers (EANs) in Europe, and the GTIN nomenclature has been expanded to cartons as well. For example the GTIN-12 (formerly known as the Universal Product Code or UPC in the United States) and the GTIN-13 (formerly known as the European Article Number or EAN in Europe), which share a common symbology, are traditionally used for identifying single items (as is the GTIN-8), whereas the GTIN-14 (formerly known as the Interleaved 2 of 5 (I2of5) in the United States though the I2of5 symbology is still used) is traditionally used to identify multiples of a single item such as a carton quantity of a particular GTIN-12 or GTIN-13 item.

If the enterprise decides to incorporate RFID, what frequency is appropriate to use? Likely the RFID tags would be passive (no onboard energy source) versus active (equipped with an energy source) though this would be dependent upon the industry and purpose of the tagging. One of the significant impediments to RFID implementation across sectors such as retail has been the cost of the RFID tag itself: passive tags being priced lower than active tags with the difference being the onboard energy source. With passive tags the RFID reader's own energy activates the tag to send a signal back to the RFID reader, whereas an active tag with an onboard energy source can send its signal to the RFID reader from a greater distance than a passive tag is capable of doing. In distribution centers the close proximity of the RFID reader to the items and cartons (and pallets) likely does not warrant the use of active tags and their cost would be prohibitive due to the volume of items, cartons, and pallets to be tagged even with the economy of scale. In some supply chains, such as retail, the very cost of some items does not warrant an expensive active RFID tag. The active RFID tag may be priced as much or higher than some low-cost items such as a package of disposable pens.

There are subtleties involved in printing barcode labels—adhesive, coating, media, and methodology—that customer enterprises must not leave to the decision of their vendors. The ability of the label to survive the journey and survive in the environment is two different scenarios entirely and will be explored more in the third part of the book.

Enable

There is a distinct difference between educating and enabling, whereby the former is providing knowledge and information, the latter is providing the ability to make something possible or easy. Educating the vendor community about what the customer enterprise requires and how supply chain concepts work will not necessarily make them able to implement the needed solutions. Nor will simply sending the vendors to the eB2B solution vendor purely solve the problem: eB2B is only one facet of vendor compliance. Education is a start but it is not a solution.

Consider that some of the simplest needs may have the simplest solutions, such as where to find a barcode label and ribbon provider, and what are suggested barcode printers and software for different operating systems. In my experience most customer enterprises are loathe to get involved in just publishing a list of companies for fear of repercussion from vendors should there be a bad experience with a company on the list. Yet partnering with national barcode software and hardware companies who can refer to local qualified resellers for vendors who have no resources of their own would at least help enable those vendors who are without the expertise to implement the necessary technology. Customer enterprises seem to have no trouble whatsoever in naming their eB2B vendors—they have little choice because they typically outsource the technology enrollment to those eB2B companies as well—but otherwise vendors are left without resources. Similarly customer enterprises specify their transportation carriers thus leaving their vendors with no other options. If there are special tags, hangars, fill material, cartons, or other requirements for your vendors, forge some strategic relationships and name the sources for your vendors and help enable the vendor community to comply with your requirements without the need for extensive or exhaustive non-value-added communications. Because of the amount of business available, working with one or more national companies on barcode or RFID tag solutions, and utilizing their partner networks, helps enable vendors who are without qualified resources. Removing the roadblocks to vendors' success in achieving vendor compliance requirements implementation should be the responsibility of the customer enterprise.

Vendor enablement means providing the knowledge (education) and tools necessary to allow the vendor community to implement the solutions required to comply with the mandates of the customer enterprise. Knowing what the result is supposed to be but not knowing how to achieve it is not enablement, for a vendor it is exasperating. For each of the vendor compliance requirements the customer enterprise should ask itself whether it has provided the education and enablement so a vendor can implement the solution on its own and achieve success. Feedback from the vendor community will allow the customer enterprise to know the answer to questions such as these. This is a perfect segue to the next Essential Element: Engage.

Engage

Vendor compliance should not be a one-way communication, nor should it be limited to the bare necessities of business: from the outset vendors should know they have the ability and opportunity to have their voices heard in meaningful conversations to discuss concerns and questions. Likewise vendor compliance should evolve to being more about just the basic business transactions of "now" and grow to providing forecast and sales data to the vendor community. Engaging the vendor community means more than just talking to them, it means conversing with them. The communication should be bi-directional and the content should broach deeper than the surface of the supply chain relationship.

If readers are in a sudden quandary when they see that my take on engagement is contradictory to my stance of minimizing vendor communications in order to reduce the operating costs of the vendor compliance program then there is a big point that is being missed. Doing a poor job in the vendor compliance documentation of explaining to the vendors what the requirements are, resulting in the vendors barraging the vendor compliance team and customer enterprise's departments with the same basic questions because they do not understand what they are being asked to do is a failure by the customer enterprise to clearly write to the audience, and this is one big way in which operating costs (and frustrations on both sides) increase. Well-run vendor compliance programs should have minimal communications from vendors on this front; vendors should be able to understand what is being asked of them and have the instructions as to how to implement the requirements at-the-ready and be easily understood.

By leveraging vendor engagement the customer enterprise has the opportunity to learn from its vendors where it has not been clear in its instructions, where its Internet portal has a functional failure, or where one of its own service providers (e.g. the eB2B service company) is not meeting performance expectations. The customer enterprise can leverage its vendor community in a check-and-balance relationship to help itself monitor its own performance metrics and supply chain aspects, essentially utilizing a workforce at no cost to itself.

Some readers may scoff at the notion that a small vendor can teach a large customer enterprise new tricks. However, my own experience proves that to be incorrect: on behalf of several vendor clients I have navigated unique situations and negotiated favorable resolutions with national U.S. customer enterprises to creatively solve some unique supply chain conditions that fell outside the normal vendor compliance parameters. The only issue is that some buying organizations are more receptive to working with their vendor communities than others.

Vendor engagement moves beyond the basic business transactions by—eventually—providing vendors with accurate forecast and sales data. The latter—sales data—by product and by geography (e.g. the store level so that with a store address listing the vendor can perform geographical analysis by product) within a reasonable time period (e.g. weekly for retail), is based on what the customer enterprise has purchased and subsequently sold or consumed per vendor. Sales data should be relatively easy to provide to vendors in an early phase of the vendor compliance program. Forecast data is of little use unless it is very accurate, a burden which falls squarely on the shoulders of the customer enterprise. Phasing in forecast data based on purchase history would at least be a starting point and, when provided early enough, would allow vendors to make planned purchases of raw materials in advance. Keep in mind that forecasts may be considered a commitment so be wary of locking vendors into financial situations based on your forecasts only to lower quantities later or cancel the forecasts and future orders all together. Ensure the forecast data is clearly defined so vendors know if it is accurate whereby action can or should be taken against the data provided.

Companies often like to talk about their "open door" policies in regards to how their employees can freely discuss matters with executives, but how many customer enterprises have the same policy with their vendors? Yet what if a vendor could reduce the cost of a relationship while maintaining or increasing its own sales: shouldn't a customer enterprise be at least willing to listen? Engaging with vendors by providing them the data they need to make informed decisions may be akin to or result in outsourcing a cost-reduction or product sales or marketing analysis, something that should interest every buying enterprise. Some vendors may be industry experts and can offer experienced insights that can lead to new product ideas, new sales concepts, or improved processes.

Examine

The examination of vendor performance enables the customer enterprise to determine whether a vendor is either conforming to the compliance mandates or is disruptive to supply chain operations (and therefore likely adding costs), and possibly also whether the vendor presents a risk (e.g. is near to business failure or the disruptions are having a ripple effect across the supply chain). Performance and risk determination relies on the establishment of metrics, the assignment of key performance indicators, and the analysis as the vendor scorecard.

Metrics are the measurements against which performance is judged. Common supply chain metrics are order acceptance or rejection (the percentage of purchase orders accepted or rejected by the vendor); percentage of backorders; shipment accuracy (e.g. the right items in the right quantities); invoice accuracy (only billing for the shipped items for the shipped quantities) and invoice timeliness (the invoice should not be sent before the shipment nor should it be sent too long after the shipment); and quality inspection results.

Key Performance Indicators are the level of performance against a metric. For example, if 100 purchase orders are sent to a vendor in a given month and 90 are accepted, the key performance indicator (KPI) of purchase order acceptance for that vendor for that month would be 90 percent.

The *scorecard* is the graded performance of the KPI: this is the determination as to whether the KPI is, simply, good or bad, on a metric-by-metric basis. Some scorecards translate the KPI into a grade much like many of us were used to receiving on our school report cards, e.g. A, B, C, D, and F where an A grade would be (for example) a KPI of 90 percent to 100 percent. The scorecard for one metric may be different than that for another metric. For example a 90 percent backorder rate may be less than desirable and thus be assigned a grade of C but a 90 percent invoice timeliness to shipment rate may be acceptable and receive a grade of A.

Based on a vendor's performance the cycle of how often a metric is analyzed may change. During the initial months of a vendor relationship it is likely that the vendor's performance is monitored very closely, e.g. performance is scored regularly (e.g. weekly or monthly) based on the number of transactions and frequency of transactions within a given time period. But if the vendor proves consistently high performance the cycle of analysis may increase, say from monthly to quarterly. Conversely a poor performing vendor or a vendor whose performance is degrading would see their cycle compress from quarterly to monthly. By managing the exceptions and highlighting only the underperforming vendors the compliance team can focus on addressing the problematic performers who are causing disruptions to the supply chain and whose poor performance is likely adding costs to operations.

While it is always important to provide key performance indicator data feedback on vendor performance to both the vendor and those inside the customer enterprise who monitor vendor performance, the cycle within which the metric is scored can be variable in length depending upon performance factors. Focusing on the scorecards and not the key performance indicators is one way of dividing-and-conquering the problem of managing vendor performance by exception.

Enforcement

What can—or should—the customer enterprise do when a vendor does not comply with the vendor compliance requirements? Are there exemptions for first-time offenders or waivers for vendors with good track records? The issue of *chargebacks*—financial penalties for non-compliance—is a sticky one at best and the subject of much heated debate within some industries such as U.S. retail, where vendors have charged that retailers use chargebacks as a profit center and that chargeback amounts are in clear excess of the cost of the correction.

First and foremost in my opinion the customer enterprise must accept its full responsibility as judge, jury, and executioner in this trading partner relationship and as such its precise ability to examine without error is the only way to guarantee full fairness before levying a financial penalty. Because 100 percent veracity is likely impossible the customer enterprise must be willing to yield that it may sometimes be wrong. And now with even the smallest margin of error existing there is room for reasonable discussion.

Some vendor compliance programs may forgive first-offenders: this would make sense given that, even after testing, if something is going to go wrong it probably will during the first live exchange of information. I have experienced several vendor compliance programs that waive financial penalties if the vendors maintain high, though not necessarily unachievable, performance levels. This goal-setting methodology makes the vendor engaged in the chargeback reduction exercise by maintaining high performance indicators, and the customer enterprise sends the signal that "to err is human" or otherwise saying that we all make mistakes and if you do we won't penalize you as long as your performance level is high and yet attainable.

The ability to financially penalize vendors by withholding money from invoice payments for the failure to comply with vendor compliance requirements has some grounds within the U.S. Uniform Commercial Code and will be reviewed in more detail later in the book. I am not opposed to reasonable financial penalties for non-compliance if and only if the customer enterprise has done its full responsibility in explaining and educating and enabling and examining. The problem is that too often the customer enterprise has failed in its trading partner relationship obligations and the financial penalties are so excessively beyond the reasonable cost of the correction that they must truly be for the sake of profits.

Empathy

Once you have completed the list of everything you are going to have your vendors do, and set the bar at the level you expect your vendors to perform, step back and place yourself in the perspective of your vendors across the entire demographic. How would you feel about being handed the vendor compliance requirements written by your enterprise and being told you had to comply with them or face financial penalties for non-compliance?

Are you able to sympathize with your vendors regarding the extra costs being imposed on them? Are you being fair in providing sufficient time to implement the requirements, being considerate of the time of year, waiting until a lull in your industry's business cycle, or after your industry's major conference that everyone has spent several weeks if not months gearing up for in preparation? Are all the resources readily available to allow the vendor to self-implement the requirements? Is the documentation written clearly and easy to understand?

The customer enterprise should ensure that the lead business transaction that initiates the supply chain activity between itself and its vendors contains sufficient information to allow the vendor to process the transaction to its completion. The operational directives being demanded upon the vendors should make sense and not contradict themselves at different points in the compliance documentation. Are all the questions answered and the gaps covered and closed? If the vendor does have a question are there clear points of contact specific to different topics, e.g. accounting, technical, logistics, and general compliance?

Depending upon the industry and the customer enterprise's place in it, empathy for its vendors may not enter the equation because the belief in business is all about the bottom line. But for customer enterprises that want to do a better job of embracing their vendors and controlling their own costs, taking a second look at what they are going to be demanding their vendors to do may very well be the difference between engaged vendors and enraged vendors. Before you publish the next vendor compliance requirement, take a breath, take a step back, put yourself in the place of a typical vendor, and consider if what has been defined and done was the best possible, and that the vendor community is not being trodden upon unfairly.

Equality and Ethics

The two topics of equality and ethics are so closely intertwined that it makes sense to discuss them together. Vendors should all be treated equally because it is just the ethical thing to do. In terms of vendor compliance, this can have a direct relationship on the assessment of chargebacks.

It would be grossly unfair to waive financial penalties for non-compliance for one vendor because that vendor is large and a lot of business is conducted with them or in favor of better pricing or other preferential treatment that smaller vendors are not able to provide; in fact it would be unethical to allow this to occur. Similarly one vendor should not be given preferential treatment to secure a brand label or favorable inventory allocations. The rules and requirements of vendor compliance must be applied to all vendors equally, without distinction or favoritism.

Remember that the purpose of chargebacks is to bring disruptive vendors into compliance. Large vendors that are non-compliant are probably causing large disruptions which translate into large costs borne to the customer enterprise. Chargeback assessment should be objective, not subjective, when it comes to which vendors are penalized for their non-compliance. All vendors are equal when it comes to vendor compliance rules and requirements.

Extend

Once you have reached this point in the list of essential elements you can seek to extend vendor compliance through the internal relationships of the enterprise, rather than just having it govern an external customer-vendor relationship.

In my first book, *Detecting and Reducing Supply Chain Fraud* published by Gower Publishing in August 2012, I defined the supply chain as "The movement of something between a customer and a supplier from start to finish." The *something* can be anything such as raw materials, components, finished goods, money, services, data or information (the latter being the more intelligent version of the former), or documentation. What makes up a "customer" and a "supplier" is open to interpretation. In traditional vendor compliance trading partner relationships the customer (buying) enterprise is separate and distinct from the vendor (selling) enterprise. But the notion of the internal customer-supplier relationship has existed for a very long time: the human resources department is an internal supplier of services to the rest of the enterprise, and the other departments of the enterprise are the customers of the information technology department who provides both goods (e.g. computers) and services (e.g. virus protection, e-mail, network support, Internet access). So why cannot vendor compliance apply to an internal customer-supplier relationship? The answer is that it can.

A catalyst event is required to bring the supply chain to life. Whether it is a demand due to an out-of-stock situation or the next process in a chain of events as with a financial loan package that must follow certain steps for qualification, either the pull or push through the chain of events is causing activity and this activity is causing the *something* to move. Whatever the *something* is it moves from someone or somewhere that is supplying it (the "supplier") to someone or somewhere that is receiving it (the "customer"). The same responsibilities hold true of the external supplier as for the internal supplier: the something being moved should be the right thing in the right quantity and in first quality condition. Any failure should result in a penalty to the supplier. If internal departments were penalized for the mistakes they caused and the (non-value-added) wastefulness that was the result it is likely that more focus would be on getting everything right the first time before passing it along.

Metrics, key performance indicators, and scorecards can be established for exactly the same purpose as are done for traditional customer-vendor trading partner relationships. Metrics to measure accuracy, throughput, quality, and redundant efforts (e.g. rework) are just as applicable to internal relationships as they are to external relationships. The internal scorecard can be used to identify bottleneck processes and departments, ineffective procedures, and training or skills gaps. Where vendor compliance documentation informs external entities how to engage with the customer enterprise, Sarbanes-Oxley, ISO (International Organization for Standardization), and standard operating procedures documentation can inform internal customers and suppliers how to interact with each other in the internal enterprise supply chain. But just documentation is not enough without the key essential elements that have been discussed here.

Evolve

The key technologies used in vendor compliance are barcode scanning, electronic business-to-business, and an enterprise resource planning system. These technologies—which so very many enterprises in so many global supply chains rely upon—are decades old, having been born in the 1960s, 1970s, and 1980s. And yet despite attempts to displace them, (XML was rumored to be the EDI-killer for a while, just as RFID was going to send barcodes by the wayside), these three technologies are absolutely rooted in the very core of what makes supply chains function today.

But even though global supply chains run on what could easily be branded as archaic technology it does not mean they have not evolved. These technologies work better today than they ever have: faster, more accurate, more reliable, and more secure. New operational techniques and methods have been developed into current best practices.

For the customer enterprise its vendor compliance program must continue to evolve from where it began, adding transactions and business processes, examining what works well and what does not work well, constantly improving and becoming better. For vendor enterprises that must react to their customers, the evolution will be everlasting as the business must always implement a new requirement or make changes as customers change. Vendors can learn from their customers and utilize what they are being instructed to do to their advantage, so they have an opportunity to grow technically and operationally too.

Summary

The Essential Elements is meant to be a checklist for customer enterprises seeking to establish a vendor compliance program or uncover gaps or weaknesses in existing initiatives. Taken in order the list guides one through how to build the program from conception through implementation, both externally and internally. The journey of vendor compliance for both the customer and vendor enterprise is an introspective look at how the enterprise operates and an opportunity to improve upon the weak areas that are inefficient or ineffective. The returns-on-investment are a better running enterprise with a more resilient supply chain through a closer collaboration with the vendor community. With reduced risk the enterprise is better prepared for adverse situations, such as economic, weather-related, or geopolitical. Embracing vendors as valued stakeholders and not adversaries makes the links of the supply chain stronger. Vendor compliance programs will face some adversity from the vendor community upon implementation as the vendors are forced to incur costs. Showing the vendors the whys and the benefits will help them come aboard with fewer objections. Having a well-managed vendor compliance program in place will ensure your vendors come aboard with less frustrations and lower costs for both the customer enterprise and the vendor community alike, starting the relationship off right.

PART 2

Building the Program

Introduction

In the first part of the book the Essential Elements provided a list of key characteristics representative of a successful vendor compliance program, but they symbolize only the highlights of the framework. In the second part of the book I will use these essential elements and build the foundations of the program's structure. Vendor compliance encompasses the entirety of how an enterprise operates; therefore a vendor compliance program will touch upon various operational aspects (such as legal, human resources, vendor relationship, vendor performance, and processes) and technologies (both hardware and software) used to support how the enterprise functions.

The vendor compliance program is a significant part of both supplier relationship management and supplier risk management. Supplier relationship management encompasses the total of all interactions between the customer enterprise and its suppliers (a.k.a. vendors), including business process and software systems. It spans from the interview with prospects that have something to sell, to the mentoring of the struggling suppliers, to the awarding of the achievers, to the dispatch of the non-performers. Supplier relationship management ensures compliance with child labor and product performance laws at state and federal levels, and includes ensuring no international business is conducted with individuals or enterprises on federal government restricted lists.

Inasmuch as supplier relationship management reviews the performance of suppliers to benchmarks set by the customer enterprise which can be indicators of a current or pending problem with a supplier, supplier risk management programs focus on a broader spectrum of characteristics in reviewing the risk factors in dealing with a potential supplier and the continued relationship with a current supplier. Geopolitical situations and weather-related interruptions are just two factors that can cause chaos to supply chain operations. The geographical location of a supplier in respect to the customer enterprise can be a criteria used as a basis for selection when seeking to minimize risk of supply chain disruption. Notwithstanding the factors that are beyond the control and monitoring of the customer enterprise, the ability to analyze the performance of a supplier across a variety of benchmarks provides visibility into the vendor's current state (e.g. conforming versus disruptive) at various supply chain points, and thus provides insights into the vendor's stability and capability as an ongoing trading partner.

For readers who are familiar with the term, I equate "global trade compliance" to vendor compliance across country borders. Global trade compliance (GTC) has all of the same document transaction, barcode labeling, product preparation, documentation, and legal liability considerations of vendor compliance. With GTC there is an additional focus on the supplier risk profile due to the country location and distance of the supplier. There may also be more in-depth focus to the first level supplier's own supply chain when dealing with foreign entities.

Supply chain vendor compliance is a key component, if not at the center, of both supplier relationship management and supplier risk management. Establishing an effective and well-run vendor compliance program is, in my opinion, a necessity before venturing out to tackle the larger goals of supplier relationship management and supplier risk management. And because I believe it is at the core of both of these larger initiatives it is only appropriate that I begin the examination of the vendor compliance program at what I believe should be its own core, at least in the United States, which is a legal framework that creates a foundation for an effective vendor compliance program to be built upon.

A Legal Framework

Note: I am not a lawyer or a barrister and I cannot be relied upon for legal advice.

A customer's vendors should sign a statement that they have received, read, understand, and agree to comply with the terms and conditions of the vender compliance documentation. This is necessary for several reasons. First it helps to remove any doubt that the vendor was consciously aware of the vendor compliance requirements, making it difficult to later claim ignorance of the requirements. Second, and similarly, the vendor acknowledges awareness of any financial penalties for non-compliance, something that will be discussed later in the book. Third, at its core, the rules and requirements of a vendor compliance program represent a legally binding relationship between the customer and the vendor and legally-bound relationships are recognized in signature by both parties. The vendor, in freely and knowingly entering into the business relationship with the customer in agreeing to sell its goods to the customer, does so under the terms and conditions of the vendor compliance program's rules and requirements, and this acknowledgement is memorialized in writing by signatures on the document. Any disputes to be settled — possibly in a court of law — will use this signed document that the customer and vendor acknowledged is the basis for their business relationship.

Because this is a legally-binding relationship, terminology in the documentation matters. Is what is being created a vendor compliance *agreement* or a vendor compliance *contract*? Is the person representing the customer enterprise a *buyer in the ordinary course of business* or a *purchaser*? Is the customer promoting *standards* or *guidelines* in the vendor compliance documentation? Depending upon the country or region it might be a very important distinction especially if a customer-vendor dispute necessitated mediation or ended up in a court of law.

In the United States in 1892 — at the recommendation of the American Bar Association — the National Conference of Commissioners on Uniform State Laws (NCCUSL, www.uniformlawcommission.org) was established. The NCCUSL is composed of legal practitioners such as lawyers and judges from each state who are appointed by each state's government. In the U.S. each state is granted broad authority over what happens within its borders provided the state laws do not conflict with federal laws. The purpose of the NCCUSL is to draft legislation that permits intra-state consistency while also keeping true to each state's unique jurisdiction over activities within its own borders, and all with respect to the laws of the federal government. The Uniform Commercial Code (UCC), which focuses on commercial transactions, is one of the acts the NCCUSL is responsible for creating. Cornell University Law School has an excellent web site dedicated to the UCC at http://www.law.cornell.edu/ucc.

Article I (General Provisions) Section 201 (General Definitions) of the UCC contains terms (such as "agreement," "contract," "buyer in the ordinary course of business," and "purchaser") and their definitions. In crafting vendor compliance documentation it is important to ensure that the right terminology is used, and because these are documents that are part of a legally-binding relationship seeking guidance from applicable laws or a legal framework would be, in my opinion, very advisable.

Article II (Sales) is structured very much like the flow of what could be considered the full lifecycle of a customer-vendor relationship, beginning with the terms of the sale, through the transfer of goods from the seller to the buyer, the performance of both the seller and the buyer, and what to do should a breach occur. Using Article II as a guide would help to ensure that no part of the purchase-to-pay lifecycle is accidently omitted from the coverage in the vendor compliance documentation.

The first section of Article II deals with the subject matter and includes term definitions related to sales, e.g. "contract," "agreement," "contract for sale," "sale," "lot," "goods," "termination," and "cancellation." Terminology matters especially because of the risk of a disagreement between the customer and the vendor having to be settled through mediation or in a court of law. The buyer—the customer enterprise—is the party who is establishing the vendor compliance program and is in charge of creating the vendor compliance documentation; therefore the burden is on the customer enterprise to establish the right terminology albeit from their perspective and for their protection. For example, is the sale of goods defined as the transfer of goods from the seller to the buyer, or is the sale of goods defined as the transfer of payment for goods conveyed between seller and buyer? The distinction is significant and may vary based on different regional laws, begging the question as to whether variations in the customer enterprise's vendor compliance accord ("contract" or "agreement") may be required depending on the respective geographical locations of the customer and vendor especially if country boundaries are crossed.

The third section of Article II contains information dealing with the overall construction of the contract, and includes aspects such as open price (though it is my opinion that the price should always be specified), delivery in single versus multiple lots, express and implied warranties, and F.O.B. (Free On Board) terms. Cornell University's Law School Legal Information Institute web site (http://www.law.cornell.edu/wex) defines Free On Board as: "Designation of the passing of risk of loss of goods from seller to buyer." Specifying to vendors up to what point in the supply chain they continue to bear responsibility for their goods is not only fair but important as both trading partners—seller and buyer, vendor and customer—have a clear understanding of where their responsibilities for the goods start and finish. For any enterprise to know where its responsibilities for the goods in transit begin and end will help to dictate what insurance coverage is appropriate to have and therefore the cost to insure the goods. For the useful components that should be constructed to form a basic buyer-seller contract, this section would be an excellent guide.

The fourth section of Article II and notably paragraph 401 provides a comprehensive overview of when title passes from seller to buyer. The F.O.B. terms typically dictate this and given that the first point of paragraph 401 concludes with "... title to goods passes from the seller to the buyer in any manner and on any conditions explicitly agreed on by the parties" it is really the responsibility of the customer enterprise to specify in the vendor compliance documentation when it is that they take possession of the goods.

The fifth section of Article II covers performance, how both parties (seller and buyer) are performing with respect to the terms set forth. I would highlight paragraphs 513 (Buyer's Right to Inspection of Goods) and 515 (Preserving Evidence of Goods in Dispute) with regards to vendor performance and assessment of financial penalties (a.k.a chargebacks). This is a source of great contention between sellers and buyers, notably in the U.S. retail industry: retailers financially penalize their vendors typically without providing adequate evidence of the infraction, therefore no evidence is preserved and this leaves the seller with no ability to inspect the goods. Complicating this is usually that the geographic distance between the seller's office and the location of the goods where the infraction was reported to have happened makes it financially prohibitive for even large-scale vendors to make the necessary visits to view buyer (customer) initiated disputes. Goods also move very fast in some supply chains like retail. Goods in dispute should be held by the buyer in secure locations which protect them from further damage, albeit requiring space and inventory management of its own. This is arguably a costly endeavor though seemingly a necessity if the letter, and not just the spirit, of the Uniform Commercial Code, is to be followed.

The sixth section of Article II discusses breach of terms. This is particularly applicable to vendor performance of the potential chargeback assessment. Paragraph 602 (Manner and Effect of Rightful Rejection) requires the rejection of goods to be done within a reasonable time which is considerably subjective. Notification of the rejection from the buyer to the seller must be done "seasonally." (I have wondered if this was a typographical error and was supposed to be "reasonably" yet my review of other UCC web sites reveals that the word consistently appears as "seasonably" unless this is just the perpetuation of a mistake. On March 10, 2015 I verified, via an online post with a Cornell University librarian who stated she checked the original text, the term is in fact "seasonably" and generally refers to being performed on a timely basis.) The problem is that in some supply chains, such as retail, goods move too fast for seasonal notifications to be effective. (While seasons—Winter, Spring, Summer, and Fall—are generally defined by the months they cover, what constitutes a "reasonable" timeframe would likely have to be determined by a court of law as there is no definition of "reasonable"—nor is there a definition of "seasonable"—in the UCC.) Paragraph 606 (What Constitutes Acceptance of Goods) outlines the conditions under which the buyer accepts the seller's goods, e.g. "after a reasonable opportunity to inspect the goods," (note the word "reasonable" is used, not "seasonable"), or the buyer "fails to make an effective rejection" after the inspection. Paragraph 607 (Effect of Acceptance; Notice of Breach; Burden of Establishing Breach after Acceptance; Notice of Claim or Litigation to Person Answerable Over) specifies the burden is on the buyer to give the seller reasonable notification of a breach, e.g. the goods are not acceptable for retail sale because they are wrinkled (as in the case of apparel). In my interpretation a rejection of the goods is separate from other breaches of the terms of sale, e.g. a bad barcode label on the shipping carton which would not affect the quality of the goods inside the carton. The distinction is again important in the case of disputes settled in mediation or court if the buyer (customer enterprise) is considering the business practice of the rejection of vendor goods or is in an industry where the rejection of vendor's goods is common practice. Further, if the customer's notification of the breach is when the financial penalty for non-compliance is assessed, e.g. when the vendor gets their invoice payment and notices the payment is shorted by the chargeback amount, this may not qualify as a reasonable notification of the breach. I have witnessed some chargebacks assessed weeks or months after they purportedly occurred.

The seventh section of Article II discusses remedies for breaches. Paragraph 703 (Seller's Remedies in General) describes just as the paragraph is named: several bullet points about the seller's general rights in regards to the buyer's wrongful rejection of the goods, payment failure, or other relationship breaches. Paragraph 714 (Buyer's Damages for Breach in Regard to Accepted Goods) gives guidance towards the validity of financial penalties for non-compliance by stating "Where the buyer has accepted goods and given notification … he may recover as damages for any non-conformity of tender the loss resulting in the ordinary course of events from the seller's breach as determined in any manner which is reasonable." The paragraph also states that "The measure of damages for breach of warranty is the difference at the time and place of acceptance between the value of the goods accepted and the value they would have had if they had been as warranted, unless special circumstances show proximate damages of a different amount." The argument I view here, from a chargeback standpoint, is whether non-conformities to vendor compliance rules and requirements would have devalued the goods and therefore justified damages.

Note that Paragraph 714 allows the buyer to recover damages only in a *reasonable* manner: this seems to exclude any excessive chargeback fees or penalties that could be considered punitive in nature. And while this paragraph permits damages for "non-conformity of tender" (e.g. a non-compliant carton barcode label would seem to be permissible to include), the "measure of damages" seems to be limited to the loss of the value of goods due to the said damage. If damages (a.k.a. "chargebacks") are limited to non-conformities that devalue the goods conveyed, chargebacks for many supply chain disruptions—such as those common in the U.S. retail industry—would appear to be contradictory to this paragraph of the UCC. Are supply chain disruption damages "proximate" (closely related) to damages to goods and justify special penalties? Do any delays, minor as they may be, due to non-conformities automatically justify excessive penalty? A subsequent paragraph seems to open the case for financial penalties for what the UCC terms "consequential" damages as will be reviewed next.

Paragraph 714 of Article II further states that "incidental and consequential damages" may be recovered per Article II paragraph 715 (Buyer's Incidental and Consequential Damages) which would seem to cover the customer enterprise's administrative expenses of deduction (chargeback) management. Paragraph 715 states that " … expenses reasonably incurred in inspection, receipt, transportation and care and custody of goods rightfully rejected, any commercially reasonable charges, expenses or commissions in connection with effecting cover and any other reasonable expense incident to the delay or other breach." These are activities that can be associated with those relating to the effects of handling a chargeback situation, including the physical handling of the carton or goods. If the customer enterprise were to retain as evidence the goods in question, it seems that the related expenses could be charged back to the vendor for "care and custody." Also included in Paragraph 715 are consequential damages as a result of the seller's breach that include "any loss resulting from general or particular requirements and needs of which the seller at the time of contracting had reason to know and which could not reasonably be prevented by cover[1] or otherwise." Again, and I am not a legal practitioner, but one interpretation could infer that this part opens the door to financial penalties for non-compliance to damages other than those that affect the merchantability of the goods, e.g. a bad barcode label on the carton, based on the fact that the seller (vendor) knew of the vendor compliance requirements, as evidenced by the signature of both parties on the documentation at the

---

1   "Cover refers to an act to mitigate damages by a buyer when there has been a breach of a contract by a seller. It usually refers to a situation where a seller has agreed to sell goods to a buyer and fails to perform. The buyer may have a duty to 'cover' by purchasing substitute goods to stem losses suffered. The buyer must not make any unreasonable or bad faith attempts to purchase substitute goods. In the case of cover, the buyer is entitled to damages of the difference between the contract goods and the substitute goods, plus incidental and consequential damages, but less any expenses saved due to the breach by the seller." Source: www.uslegal.com, May 2015.

beginning of the relationship. But note that only "expenses *reasonably* occurred" and "any commercially *reasonable* charges" may be levied.

Paragraph 717 (Deduction of Damages from the Price) would seem to enable the customer to deduct the damages from the invoice payment, essentially from the price of the goods still due to the buyer. But the customer enterprise is not—despite what they may see others do or what they may desire to do—free to over-penalize beyond the cost of the correction based on my interpretation of Article II's paragraph 718 (Liquidation or Limitation of Damages; Deposits) which states that "Damages for breach by either party may be liquidated in the agreement but only at an amount which is reasonable in the light of the anticipated or actual harm caused by the breach, the difficulties of proof of loss, and the inconvenience or non-feasibility of otherwise obtaining an adequate remedy. A term fixing unreasonably large liquidated damages is void as a penalty." This seems to support Article II Paragraph 714 whereby the buyer may recover damages in a *reasonable* manner and therefore seemingly prohibits punitive fees beyond the actual cost of the correction. This brings us back to the treatment of vendors ethically, and I should include, legally too. So while the UCC seems to support financial penalties for damages that directly impact the value of the goods conveyed, those that cause supply chain disruptions, and the administrative expenses of managing said damages, there would seem to be a prohibition on excessive financial penalties beyond a definable and calculable limit that would be deemed unreasonable.

Article VII (Documents of Title) should be of particular interest to many enterprises as its paragraphs focus on the standard transactions and documents used in warehouse and distribution center operations: warehouse receipts and the bill of lading document. The U.S. retail industry by-and-large uses the bill of lading format established by the group formerly known as Voluntary Interindustry Commerce Solutions (VICS) until its merger with GS1-US in 2013 and established as the GS1-US Apparel/General Merchandise group. A search on the GS1-US web site (www.gs1us.org) for "bill of lading" will yield the specification document.

The Uniform Commercial Code provides a legal foundation for the customer-vendor (buyer-seller) relationship in the U.S. and helps to establish the parameters for aspects of vendor compliance such as performance and chargebacks. For businesses outside of the United States the UCC offers a solid framework for customer enterprises to follow from which they can use to build their documents and vendor compliance program structure from a legal definition standpoint.

Vendor Compliance Documentation

There are no standards in the United States for the format of vendor compliance documentation. I recall I was contacted by a company back in 2004 with a business model and web capabilities to create standard format vendor compliance documentation but unfortunately the company could garner no traction and it soon went out of existence. It was certainly a worthwhile idea that would have been beneficial to vendors in any industry but it could not succeed without customer enterprise support. Companies seem content to create their documentation their own way without guidelines or standards within any industry that I have encountered, thus further frustrating vendors who must discern the same information from documents of different formats. New customer entrants to vendor compliance programs tend to copy what the older, larger industry players have been doing, perpetuating their faulty formats.

As mentioned in the Essential Elements review there are — or can be — several documents that together embody the whole of a vendor compliance program. Because there are no standards a customer enterprise can create a single document or separate the contents across different documents. In general it makes more sense to divide the material by subject matter to prevent having a single unnecessarily large document. It will be easier and more acceptable for the vendors to digest. Issuing less-frequent specific updates to smaller, subject-matter documents as the updates are necessary rather than numerous repeated updates to a single comprehensive document will be less confusing to the vendor community. Operational instructions and technical information should be divided into different documents; technical specifications (e.g. schematic drawings of labels) can be their own document and not necessarily included in an operational "how-to" document. The customer should put themselves in a vendor's position as to how a vendor would use and distribute their documentation, e.g. technical information to the information technology staff, routing information to the distribution center, general vendor compliance information to a key contact person, and chargeback information to the accounting and operations departments. So the customer should divide the documentation conducive to how it will be used by its vendor community and how it might be used internally. Remember: empathize with what you are demanding your vendors to do, and that includes how you are formatting and dividing the information you are presenting for maximum readability, flexibility, and usability.

Vendor Compliance Manual

The vendor compliance manual can serve a broad, general purpose in introducing the concept of vendor compliance to the vendor community and provide some "how-to" guidance. There should be some statement from the customer as to why the vendor compliance program, or why certain vendor compliance program initiatives (e.g. radio frequency identification) are being implemented. Vendors will likely know that the compliance program is to save the customer money, so the statement from the customer should explain the cost-benefit advantages for both trading partners and why the investment both trading partners are making will improve the relationship. If an initiative will help increase throughput or reduce an error rate than say so.

Basic policies and procedures should be outlined in this document. The customer enterprise should outline its commitment to ethics and the fair and balanced treatment of all of its vendors. Prohibition against child labor, cautions against hazardous materials, requirements of vendors to be properly licensed (based on local jurisdictions) and insured, the customer's return policy, and a no-gift-giving or a restricted gift policy would all be advisable statements to consider for inclusion. The customer enterprise's holiday and closing schedule calendar for the year should be included so vendors know the days the customer's contacts will not be available. If office closing schedules will differ from distribution center closing schedules this should be detailed.

Vendors need to know eB2B mailbox information and eB2B network provider or file transfer options for electronic business-to-business communications. If vendors are already engaged with paper documents or are permitted to begin their trading partner relationships exchanging paper documents, how-to instructions for paper-electronic parallel testing and migration from paper to electronic communications must be stated. The schedule (days and times) for drop-off and pickup of eB2B transactions would be helpful. For example, stating that purchase orders are delivered once every work day (Monday through Friday) between the hours of 1:00 AM and 5:00 AM Eastern Standard Time (U.S.), or the inbound mailbox that includes the pickup of invoices and advance ship notices is cycled every 30 minutes 24/7.

Some retailers with physical stores in the United States rely on goods being delivered "floor-ready" by the vendor. The term "floor-ready" can mean any combination of free of wrinkles, item and price tagged, the clothing already on a customer-specified hanger, poly-bagged, or folded in a certain way—the goal being to be able to take the item from the shipping carton and place it directly on the sales floor without any other intervention. To help facilitate the goal of "floor-ready" some retailers will restrict the materials that can be used to fill the empty carton space (known as "fill material") which itself requires the retailer to handle and either stockpile for reuse or dispose of, thus resulting in incurred costs. Large items such as mattresses and bicycles and furniture require special handling as do small expensive items like jewelry and watches and certain electronics. Consider placing special handling information for your industry in the vendor compliance manual unless the content is sufficiently detailed to justify a separate document of its own.

A list of key contacts can be included in the vendor compliance manual or in a separate document. Telephone numbers, mailing addresses, and e-mail addresses for contact persons covering accounting, technology, buying, and vendor relations at the corporate level, and the same (telephone and e-mail addresses) for regional warehouse (a.k.a. distribution center) managers. The location of the regional warehouses (physical addresses, main telephone numbers, and identification codes) would also be appropriate and can be combined with the key contact information in a separate document or included in the main vendor compliance manual.

ROUTING GUIDE

The routing guide helps vendors select the designated ground carriers to use based on the ship-from location and ship-to destination and the size of the shipment (e.g. small package, less-than-truckload, full truckload). Likely the customer has already set up accounts with the designated ground carriers and is directing the vendors to bill against the customer's accounts rather than bill against the vendor accounts and submit the freight charges to the customer: this alleviates any up-charging (profiting) by the vendor and helps the customer negotiate better rates with the carriers due to economy of scale. Because not all common carriers cover all ground routes select carriers may be required based on the ship-from and ship-to points. Likewise not all carriers handle all types of shipment sizes so multiple carriers per ground route may be required.

The advanced scheduling of the carrier pickup by the vendor is critical to ensure sufficient time for the carrier to add the vendor's ship-from location to the route for the desired or available pick-up day. Some customer enterprises use a third-party to handle all shipment scheduling activity while others require their vendors to coordinate individually with the different carriers. Routing requests and instructions can be handled via eB2B transactions or via web-based portals. The shipment scheduling is important for the customer enterprise also because it helps to prevent a delivery traffic jam at the ship-to destinations.

If air, train, or ship transportation is a part of the customer enterprise's regular supply chain, this routing information will also have to be included. This goes back to the F.O.B. (Free On Board) statement in the vendor compliance documentation as to who is responsible for—who owns the goods—until what point in transit? If the vendor is responsible for these longer journeys than the customer enterprise does not need to dictate preferred carriers or scheduling. However if the customer enterprise is accepting responsibility for (ownership of) the goods earlier, e.g. at the point of air, train, or ship terminal, the customer should clearly specify transfer terms and instructions in the vendor compliance documentation.

DATA MAPPING GUIDE

Electronic Data Interchange (EDI) in the United States is something of a "non-standard standard" when it comes to the variety of ways some information can be represented within the same document (business transaction, e.g. a purchase order). For example in the Purchase Order (EDI document number 850) either the purchase order's ship date window or delivery date window can be provided. There can be little defined difference to a vendor as to designating when a purchase order may ship from their facility or when it can arrive at a customer's facility; in fact because the vendor has little control over the customer's common carrier journey I believe most vendors would prefer to be simply told the date range when the purchase order can leave their facility (the ship date). Yet both date range types (ship versus delivery) are able to be sent.

The argument that the date qualifier codes in EDI differentiate the date types (the ship date codes, which can be sent individually or in pair, are 037 for Ship Not Before and 038 for Ship Not Later Than; the delivery date codes, which can be sent individually or in pair, are 063 for Do Not Deliver After and 064 for Do Not Deliver Before), is a little meaningless considering that vendors use fairly common ERP systems that may lack the advanced—and sometimes custom—capabilities of the advanced ERP systems used by customer enterprises. This is especially true for small, mid-size, and even large vendors using more mid-range ERP systems that have not undergone modifications or enhancements. Customers should consider the demographics of its vendor community and judge the vendor community's capabilities before dictating unachievable requirements, and this includes down to the data level. Choosing common sense data elements to send to vendors will only help close any confusion or capability gaps.

The data-mapping guide shows the vendor what data records and data fields (known as "data segments" and "data elements" in EDI parlance) will be required and the field attributes, e.g. character (alphanumeric) versus numeric, total size, number of decimal places. Realistic samples of final output covering different scenarios are very helpful for vendors to follow. A stock fulfillment (ship to a distribution center) purchase order will probably be slightly differently structured than a drop-ship (direct to consumer) purchase order. If the customer enterprise has the option of sending both then examples of both should be detailed in the documentation.

CHARGEBACK FEES

Deductions for compliance violations is going to be a sensitive enough topic with the vendor community already, so taking time to clearly document the reasons—and resolutions—is advisable. I have read too many vendor compliance documents where the chargebacks—also called "expense offsets"—were described so vaguely that multiple descriptions could have applied to a single violation. If a customer is going to withhold money from a vendor as judge and jury then the explanation should be clear.

Separating the chargeback list into functional type is an organizational help. Technology chargebacks would include those related to incorrect data mapping, though simply stating "incorrect data mapping" is too broad and is just one generic chargeback. Specifically there are operational aspects of the technology relationship, such as invoices that do not match purchase orders and ship notices, or invoices sent beyond a specific number of days after a shipment is sent, that can be analyzed for compliance. A document with a structure problem such as an improperly formatted data segment (data record) could result in a chargeback. Sending an eB2B document with a duplicate control number might also be another technology-related offense that causes a chargeback.

Operational issues typically found on chargeback lists include unusable barcode labels (the barcode cannot be scanned), missing barcode labels, merchandise not packaged as "floor-ready", improper bill of lading or packing list documentation, missing bill of lading or packing list documentation, unauthorized item substitution, shipment received too early or too late based on ship/delivery date range, shipping carton was too small or too large, carton was overweight, or incorrect information on carton, master-pack, or pallet barcode labels.

LABEL, TAG, CARTON SCHEMATICS

Item tags, carton and pallet labels, and radio-frequency identification tags must be specifically detailed for vendors so as to leave no doubt as to the requirements. This necessitates schematic drawings of what each label and tag is to look like. Each schematic should detail the height and width dimensions of the overall object (e.g. label or tag) and what material to be used (e.g. paper versus paper-polyester blend for labels, paper weight for item merchandise tags). Do not leave anything to the imagination of the vendors! Inasmuch as white carton and pallet labels may be assumed they should be specified unless other color labels are necessary because they serve a visual representation purpose, e.g. yellow labels follow one cross-dock path, light-blue labels follow another cross-dock path.

For each data object (e.g. ship-to name, product identifier description) on the label or tag, the font type, font size, and maximum number of digits or characters allowed should be specified. If there is a minimum amount of space desired for readability between data objects then state that as part of the requirement.

Barcodes should be identified by their symbology (e.g. UPC-A, EAN-13, Interleaved 2 of 5, Code 128), the overall object width and height, minimum "X" dimension (the minimum width of the narrow element or bar), acceptable ratios (the narrow to thick bar dimension ratios which are fixed depending on the symbology, though common ratios are 2:1, 2.5:1, 3:1), and if the human readable attribute should be printed and if so if it is above or below the barcode. (If the human readable attribute is printed, specify the acceptable font type and font size of the human readable attribute.) The minimum amount of white space between the barcode to the next closest objects is important to note because barcode scanners rely on the white space around barcodes (known as the "quiet zone") to differentiate other objects, especially lines, from the barcodes themselves and therefore ensure only the barcode is read during the scan. A recommended minimum "quiet zone" is one-quarter of an inch.

The customer enterprise should take the time and effort to fully design each and every label and tag they require their vendors to create to ensure that the specifications reflect what is able to be accomplished in reality. I have encountered customer specifications whereby the stated font or symbology could not be achieved because it did not exist as an all-purpose option, (was not readily available across the landscape of software solutions), or the number of characters in the data field exceeded the ability to create a font of the specified size. The customer enterprise must think through the data it is delivering to its vendors and the data it is receiving from its vendors and ensure its label specifications reflect the reality of the data being transacted.

Schematic drawings should also specify where the labels and tags should be placed on the item or carton or pallet, noting the variety of situations that can arise such as different carton sizes which may necessitate different label configurations and require careful planning when specifying what data goes where on the label: positioning a barcode at a place on a label where the label will be folded over the edge of a carton will make part of that barcode unusable. Depending on the need, both a portrait and a landscape configured version of the carton label may be required. However, my advice to the customer enterprise is repeated again: place yourself in the position of your vendor, having to comply with not only your vendor compliance requirements but those of other customers in the industry; minimize your exceptions and standardize your variations as much as possible. While you may not care about helping your vendors comply with the requirements of your competitors, minimizing any exception will help your vendors achieve success with your compliance requirements.

Documentation Location and Distribution

The customer enterprise may want to consider that the vendor compliance documentation is now a guidebook of competitively sensitive information and should not be made so readily available to just anyone. Posting this information to an unsecured web site may not be the wisest of decisions. The documentation should be secured behind a web portal only accessible to qualified vendor partners or can be sent via e-mail once a selling enterprise has been designated as a vendor. Due to the sensitive nature of the information, the vendor compliance manual should have a statement that none of the vendor compliance documentation is permitted to be distributed by the vendor unless it is to an employee or known third-party agent of the vendor, and that all recipients of the vendor compliance documentation are entrusted with its security and secrecy.

Transactions and Reactions

Electronic Business-To-Business (eB2B) was noted as one of the Essential Elements. What were once paper-based business documents now exist in electronic form under the standards of EDI or UN/EDIFACT or some mutually-agreed upon format. As part of its vendor compliance documentation the customer enterprise must inform its vendors as to how these electronic documents will be used, not just individually but also in relationship to each other and with regards to the timeliness of the expected reaction to a given transaction.

The customer enterprise must recognize that some part of its vendor community will likely lie outside its geographic area and may very well exist in other time and date zones. As such it is very important that the vendor compliance documentation always precisely specifies exactly when a transaction or a reaction is to occur from its own customer enterprise and time zone perspective. For example:

- "Purchase orders will be transmitted once per day between 3:00 AM and 5:00 AM Eastern Standard Time U.S."

- "Advance Ship Notices are processed every 30 minutes between 9:00 AM and 6:00 PM Greenwich Mean Time."

- "Routing Requests sent before 12:00 noon Eastern Standard Time U.S. will be processed and have Routing Instructions returned before 12:00 noon Eastern Standard Time U.S. on the next business day. Routing Requests sent after 12:00 noon Eastern Standard Time U.S. will be processed and have Routing Instructions sent before 5:00 PM Eastern Standard Time U.S. on the second business day."

> *Though my expertise is in EDI and I only have cursory experience with EDIFACT I have included references to both standards' documents in the examples below, where applicable. It is my belief that what works within EDI should work within EDIFACT as well.*

DOCUMENT ACKNOWLEDGEMENT

At the basics each business document sent by one trading partner and received by the other trading partner should be acknowledged by the receiving party. (This is the EDI Functional Acknowledgement (document number 997) or the equivalent EDIFACT CONTRL.) The purpose of the document acknowledgement is to inform the sending party at minimum that the sent document was received, but more so of any standards conformity errors with regards to the document they sent.

As mentioned previously, EDI (and perhaps this applies to EDIFACT) standards are so broad that they have become a "non-standard standard." A customer enterprise may elect to use a subset of qualifying code values for a particular data field that varies slightly from the subset of code values used by another customer enterprise. This is permissible because neither customer enterprise is going outside the standard of all defined code values. (It becomes more of a data mapping issue for the vendor to limit acceptable code values for the same data field based upon which customer trading partner's documents the vendor is processing at the time.) This also applies to data segments (data records) and data elements (data fields) within the data segments: different customer trading partners can require or optionally use certain records and fields, necessitating the custom mapping a vendor is required to do for each of its trading partners it sells to. Inasmuch as the majority of data records, and many of the data fields, will be common across industry trading partners, even a single variation necessitates exception processing by the (vendor) trading partner.

The document acknowledgement is a response to both an objective and subjective review of the inbound business transactions, verifying file structure and data values to the eB2B standard in-use (the objective review) as well as to the sending party's use of the eB2B standard (the subjective review). For example, an incorrectly formatted data segment (data record) would be flagged as being in error. An invalid value, or a value from the entire set of standard's values but one that the customer trading partner chose not to use, in a data element (data field) would result in the transaction being flagged as in error.

This filtering prevents bad data from infiltrating into the receiving enterprise's business software application (the ERP system) and causing operational chaos. Inbound documents that do not pass inspection (that result in errors) are rejected and the sending party notified via the document acknowledgement. The process of receiving a business document, objective and subjective inspection, and transmission of the document acknowledgement should all occur within 24 business hours. More on how the document acknowledgement works is covered in the third part of the book.

In the subsequent transaction and reaction descriptions I shall not include a mention of the document acknowledgement. Just know that for every document sent, except for the acknowledgement itself, a confirming document acknowledgement is expected to be received.

In EDI the Application Advice (824) is also used to communicate document errors. The Application Advice can allow more level of detail in describing the reason behind the failure than the Functional Acknowledgement for customer enterprises that want to share extra information with their vendors as to the nature of the errors detected. The more information provided to the vendors when an error occurs the less likely non-value-added communication will be necessary between the vendor and a contact at the customer enterprise.

PURCHASE ORDERS

The two popular transaction-reaction pairs for purchase orders are the purchase order — purchase order acknowledgement and the purchase order — purchase order change. The purchase order is the customer enterprise's commitment to buy goods at the quantity and price as specified in the purchase order. Payment terms and the ship or delivery date window are also commonly sent attributes of a purchase order. The purchase order acknowledgement is the vendor's opportunity to accept or reject all or part of the purchase order. Reason codes as to why each line item of the purchase order was accepted or rejected are part of the EDI standards. Reasons might be that the item is not available (e.g. not yet published, out of stock), price, or quantity discrepancies. Vendors typically must turn around purchase order acknowledgements within 24 to 48 business hours of the purchase order receipt in order to allow the customer enterprise to react accordingly, e.g. make adjustments in its enterprise software or send alerts to its own customers of anticipated product delays. However the amount of time the customer enterprise allows the vendor to respond to a purchase order with a purchase order acknowledgement is likely dependent upon different factors such as the ship or delivery date of the purchase order relative to the purchase order date, or whether there is a consumer up the supply chain waiting for an order status.

The purchase order change is the customer enterprise's alteration of a previously sent purchase order. The change may be add or subtract existing item quantities, advance or extend dates, update prices, add or delete items, or cancel the purchase order entirely, sometimes in reaction to the vendor's purchase order acknowledgement of the original purchase order. Even one change to a purchase order can wreak havoc upon a vendor's operations, causing them to scramble to advance manufacturing scheduling, bear excessive transportation costs, or add extra labor. Furthermore, because the purchase order change is an exception, it is likely that it will be handled manually and not systematically by the vendor's business software application, requiring additional time and effort to discern what changed between the original purchase order and the change order and the effect of the changes to the vendor's supply chain operations. Customer enterprises should be very wary of using purchase order changes (unless confirming a purchase order acknowledgement) and instead seek to get the purchase order correct the first time. Changes to purchase orders result in expensive disruptions to vendors' supply chain operations and represent exactly the kinds of exceptions the customer enterprise should be trying to mitigate for themselves.

The purchase order change can be sent as a stand-alone document by the customer enterprise or used as a transaction reaction to confirm a vendor's changes sent in the purchase order acknowledgement. If the customer enterprise requires their vendors to send purchase order acknowledgements, sending purchase order changes confirming those acknowledgements would allow the vendors to know their purchase order changes have been accepted and registered in the customer's business software system. This extra effort on the part of the customer enterprise to send the purchase order change confirming a vendor's purchase order acknowledgement could help alleviate unnecessary vendor communication whereby vendors contact the customer enterprise to confirm purchase order acknowledgement acceptance, thereby lowering costs due to the removal of non-value-added activity.

In EDI the Text Message transaction (EDI 864) can be used to confirm purchase order acknowledgment acceptance via a specifically formatted message. The text message transaction was used in the days (years) before e-mail to send free-format messages. Formatting specific message lines for notifications such as purchase order acknowledgement acceptance and confirmation—with a listing of the purchase order identifiers—provides the vendor with verification that their purchase order acknowledgement was accepted. This is another method of automatically communicating with the vendor, alleviating an unknown, and reducing non-value-added activities for the customer and vendor enterprises in any manual (e.g. telephone or e-mail) follow-up communications confirming the acceptance of the purchase order acknowledgement. (The EDIFACT transaction GENRAL would seem to be used for similar purposes to the EDI 864 in allowing free-form text messages to be communicated.)

SHIPMENT NOTIFICATION

Each and every shipment against a purchase order should generate a shipment notification, whether it is a shipment of one carton or many cartons, whether the shipment type is small parcel, less-than-truckload, or full truckload, or via some other transportation means (e.g. air or sea), or whether shipping complete or partial against one or many purchase orders. (The issue of whether the customer enterprise permits partial shipping of purchase orders is up to each entity.) The shipment notification lets the customer enterprise know that, to paraphrase a saying, "the goods have left the building."

When I had the opportunity to serve on the VICS TPAC committee we addressed the issue of timeliness between the goods leaving a vendor facility (either the vendor's own facility or that of a contract manufacturer or distributor) and the transmission of the shipment notification (the EDI 856, a.k.a. Advance Ship Notice). What is the ideal or maximum timeliness between these two events? In many cases vendor facilities are in close proximity to customer ship-to distribution centers whereby a truck can get there within just a few hours, sometimes even quicker.

The electronic ship notice is important because the data contained within its structure reflects each shipment's characteristics (e.g. weight and volume) and contents e.g. the purchase orders that make up the shipment, what is printed on and reflected within the pallet and master carton barcode labels (or embedded in the radio frequency identification tags) and details what items are in each carton. When the pallet and carton barcode labels are scanned (or when the radio frequency identification tags are read) upon shipment receipt, the unique identifiers in the labels and tags are compared to the data in the electronic ship notice: this is why the electronic ship notice must arrive and be processed before the physical shipment.

The VICS TPAC committee agreed that it was reasonable for vendors to send the electronic ship notice within one hour of the shipment leaving the facility, regardless of whether it was a vendor-owned facility or it was a vendor contract facility. In my experience some retailers had already begun to react to the situation of vendor facilities located nearby to their own ship-to distribution centers by establishing special electronic mailboxes for electronic ship notices that were checked every 30 to 60 minutes. I have only encountered one retailer which specified that the electronic ship notice should be sent no later than 30 minutes after the physical shipment of the goods; one hour seems to be the broader acceptable standard.

Goods traveling by air and sea may not necessitate an eB2B shipment notification within one hour of the goods having left on their journey. Nor perhaps will these methods of shipments possibly require a traditional eB2B shipment notification: perhaps an electronic form (e.g. a formatted document or spreadsheet) that the vendor completes with the shipment information and submits to the customer enterprise via e-mail will suffice. However the customer enterprise should require the vendors to alert them by some means, and on a timely basis, each time a shipment is initiated. Remember: vendor compliance is implemented in phases, e.g. domestic and then international.

INVOICES

Invoices should be based upon what was shipped (ship notices) not what was ordered (purchase orders). Invoices should not arrive before the ship notice or physical shipment. Inasmuch as it would seem to favor the customer enterprise to have vendor invoices delayed as long as possible, this payables strategy is a false one: the money is owed, it just has not been asked for yet. Invoices should be sent relatively soon after the physical shipment, e.g. within five but not more than 10 business days. This enables any discrepancies in invoiced quantities or invoiced items to be researched while the last activity (the receipt, preferably using Electronic Data Capture and audited against the ship notice and purchase order) is still relatively fresh and the data is available.

Invoice payments should be converted from paper-based (checks) to electronic via ACH (Automated Clearing House) or EFT (Electronic Funds Transfer). The cost savings from alleviating the need for check stock, envelopes, postage, and the manual labor to assemble it all together are an added benefit for the customer enterprise. Vendors will receive their payments directly into their bank accounts and no payments will be lost in the mail, thus alleviating the non-value-added communications dealing with lost checks and the wasteful activities of reissuing payments. The customer enterprise should send the corresponding eB2B payment remittance (e.g. the EDI 820, a.k.a. Payment Remittance Advice or the EDIFACT REMADV) to the vendor when the electronic payment is initiated. If the customer enterprise has affected the vendor's invoice payment via any debits or credits, an accompanying credit/debit adjustment transaction (e.g. the EDI 812) should be transmitted as well.

ROUTING INFORMATION

Vendor requests for routing information are typically a time-sensitive issue: sometimes the requests for routing instructions cannot be submitted more than 24 hours before the shipment is due to leave the facility. Because some characteristics of the routing information, such as the truck carrier, may be required on the pallet or carton barcode label, the expedited return of the routing information is critical to ensure the vendor has sufficient time to complete the preparation of the shipment. Customer enterprises should—but in my experience rarely do—consider that their vendors are smaller operations that do not run 24/7 and are located in different time zones, putting these vendors at a disadvantage when receiving delayed routing information. Vendors may be forced to pay extended time, overtime, or for additional labor to handle shipment preparation within tight schedules.

Allowing an extended amount of time greater than 24 hours (e.g. 48 business hours) prior to the shipment leaving will help alleviate some of this vendor stress. Specifying that routing requests submitted prior to 12:00 noon in the customer's time zone will be processed and answered the same day or before 12:00 noon the next business day will help vendors schedule their operations and requests accordingly. There still needs to be a constraint that prevents routing requests from being submitted too early prior to the shipment leaving, but allowing some flexibility around a noon cutoff would likely be one way of helping vendors meet a tight requirement. Customer enterprises should also do a review of what information they are requiring on the carton and pallet labels: if the carrier identity is not truly required on the label then it should be removed. Deleting unnecessary data from the carton and pallet labels that allow the vendors to create and affix the labels as early as operationally possible will result in reduced stress on the vendors' business processes.

The Operation and Transaction Supply Chain

What is it that causes supply chains to suddenly come alive in the first place? What is the catalytic event that sparks into existence all of the other linked events along the supply chain? It is very likely the need to acquire something. From a point-of-sale system, inventory system, warehouse management system, vendor managed inventory system, or any system where a participant, (be it a human or software-driven machine), upon recognizing that it has the need to acquire something and followed by the subsequent result of a mathematical calculation to determine how much to acquire, initiates an event that either sends an authorization to acquire (e.g. a purchase order) or a signal to acquire (e.g. a report, a dashboard warning, an e-mail, a text message). And from there the process of what it takes to acquire what is necessary is breathed into life.

For the customer enterprise this operation and transaction cycle encompasses the previously-discussed eB2B transactions and reactions and incorporates them into the enterprise's operational workflow. The eB2B transactions are the result of something that occurred operationally. They may have been originated by the customer or the vendor, but they are ultimately the result of the "big bang" moment that occurred at the customer enterprise when there was the need to acquire something. Each need to acquire can be thought of as a little supply chain "big bang" moment that sparks a new supply chain into existence, its lifespan running through until what could be considered the natural end of its supply chain: when payment is remitted for the invoice. (Hopefully no returns will be required.)

Leaving exceptions and functional acknowledgements off the table, a normal supply chain of transactions and reactions would look something like the following, starting with the Purchase Order, as a purchase order is one of the natural events that can be triggered from the need to acquire something. Note that the Purchase Order, PO Acknowledgement, Routing Request and Instructions, Advance Ship Notice, and Invoice are all documents transacted via eB2B. The Receiving process is notated as being performed via Electronic Data Capture (e.g. barcode and/or RFID scan) so as to acquire the data electronically.

The Quality Assurance process is an important step and one that is strategically placed in between the receipt of goods and paying the vendor's invoice. For most enterprises it would be commonplace to pay based on the receipt and not on the inspected goods, asking for a vendor credit after payment is made. Rather—and this may be dependent upon the industry—it would be preferable to pay the vendor based upon not only the accuracy of the goods received but also the quality of the goods received as determined by the Quality Assurance inspection. This alleviates the need to go back to the vendor for credits as well as improve the customer enterprise's cash position by reducing excessive vendor payments for sub-standard goods.

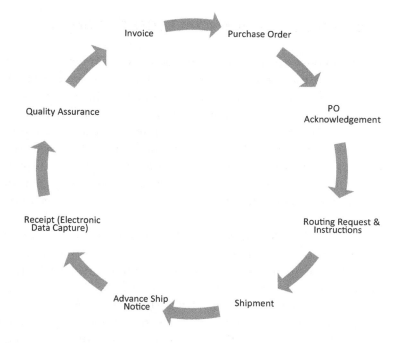

Figure 2.1   Supply Chain Transactions Cycle

Performance Monitoring

The diagram above was purposely drawn as a cycle and not a horizontal process because the acquisition of whatever is required will probably occur again and again until that something is retired. But the circular nature of the diagram also helps to envision how easy it would be to connect different transactional points together for data auditing for fraud detection and reduction (see my other book, *Detecting and Reducing Supply Chain Fraud*, Gower Publishing, 2012) or, germane to this discussion, vendor performance monitoring against established metrics used to define the vendor scorecard. Described next are some metrics commonplace in vendor compliance.

Remember that holiday closings may affect the calculation of timing metrics. If the customer enterprise does not consider holiday days as included in business hours or days, these holiday days must be excluded from calendar calculations when determining if vendors met certain compliance metrics that are date related. The same is true of weekend days (Saturdays and Sundays): are these considered business days or are these days exempt from the timing calculations?

METRIC: PURCHASE ORDER ACKNOWLEDGEMENT TIMING

This metric focuses on analyzing the number of purchase orders acknowledged outside the required turnaround timeframe. The customer enterprise should examine for patterns of exceptions such as whether the vendor is out of compliance only for purchase orders sent on Fridays, an indication that the vendor likely does not have an automated system if the purchase order acknowledgements are not sent back until the subsequent Monday or Tuesday versus a response received on Saturday. This differentiates between a turnaround time of 24 hours and 24 *business* hours, a very important distinction for the customer enterprise to establish in the vendor compliance documentation.

This becomes an issue for the customer enterprise to recognize and review for practicality, especially if it intends on penalizing vendors who fall out of compliance on this metric. For some vendors is it simply practical to only send purchase orders on a Monday, Tuesday, or Wednesday knowing that they cannot acknowledge purchase orders sent on a Thursday or a Friday on a timely basis? While at face value that statement may seem impractical from a routine supply chain standpoint, it is one that is dependent upon the industry and the vendor's products within the industry and within the customer enterprise's supply chain. I am against knowingly placing vendors in a position of financial penalty if it can be at all avoided. If the customer enterprise can reasonably modify its purchasing pattern to accommodate constraints of its vendors without compromising its own operations then neither trading partner has incurred any losses or suffered any expenses.

METRIC: PURCHASE ORDER ACKNOWLEDGEMENT PERCENTAGE

This metric analyzes the ratio of accepted, changed, and rejected line items on the purchase order. Ideally the vendor would be accepting the entire purchase order without rejections or changes assuming that there is perfect data synchronization between the trading partners; however depending upon the industry (e.g. as I learned from my experience in the publishing industry) that is not always practical. However, the goal should be a high percentage of accepted purchase order line items and lower percentages of changed and rejected purchase order line items.

Because reason codes are part of the data the vendor will return in the purchase order acknowledgement, the customer enterprise should analyze the change and reject reason codes to ascertain why vendors are changing and rejecting purchase order line items. (For example, a set of reason codes is defined within the ANSI EDI standard, and a subset of these reason codes can be used within the customer enterprise's eB2B guidelines.) The customer enterprise may learn that vendors are changing or rejecting what amounts to bad or otherwise out-of-sync data in the customer enterprise's ERP system, thus yielding insight into a system or process gap to be closed. For example, in the publishing industry vendors (publishers) send item (book) information to sellers via an ONIX data feed (http://www.editeur.org). Incorrect information from a publisher to a seller would result in the seller subsequently ordering books that are not yet ready for publication and would therefore be rejected by the publisher, all because the publisher failed to update the publication date which is a key data field sent in the ONIX data feed. A customer enterprise (a book seller) analyzing the purchase order acknowledgement reject codes from a particular publishing vendor and noting the high percentage of reject codes related to publishing date should reach out to the vendor specifically on this data issue. (It is natural in the publishing industry that publication dates will shift forward as authors and editors may run late.) The customer may be making commitments to consumers for these book titles or placing them in catalogs, on web sites, or in other marketing materials, all of which require costs to be incurred. The expense of inaccurate data is a burden shared by both trading partners.

Data inaccuracies and inconsistencies can include item prices, item order quantities (e.g. especially when items need to be ordered in standard case quantities like 12, 24, 36, or 48), item expected dates that do not align with contracted item minimum ship days, and ordering items that do not belong to the vendor to whom the purchase order was sent.

METRIC: PURCHASE ORDER ACKNOWLEDGEMENT TO RECEIPTS ACCURACY

Vendor shipment receipts should be compared against purchase order acknowledgements to analyze the accuracy of the accepted and changed line items against the shipped (and subsequently received) line items. Vendors should not be shipping line items rejected in the purchase order acknowledgement. Similarly, vendors should not be shipping original purchase order line information if either the vendor has submitted changes via the purchase order acknowledgement or the customer enterprise has submitted changes via the purchase order change. This metric therefore analyzes the vendor's ability to ship goods against the resultant purchase order after any acknowledgements and changes.

METRIC: ADVANCE SHIP NOTICE TIMELINESS TO SHIPMENT

This metric analyzes the timeless of the delivery of the Advance Ship Notice (e.g. the EDI 856) a.k.a. the electronic bill of lading to the physical delivery of the goods. The general retail industry standard—from my experience—is that the electronic ship notice should arrive at least 24 hours prior to the shipment. Most retailers do not want the electronic ship notice to arrive too soon before the shipment, such as one week or more. Traditionally this was because the data for the ship notice needed only to be active for the brief time period of the shipment receipt and data storage was an issue, so customer enterprises (such as retailers) would not commit to the ship notice data being available if it was sent by vendors too early before the physical arrival of the shipment. Even with current scalable storage capabilities, data storage still costs money and it makes sense to only keep data actively available for as long as it is required. Generally speaking it is unlikely that any vendor ship-from facility will be more than five transportation days by common road carrier from a customer enterprise's ship-to facility. With the requirement that the vendor transmit the advance ship notice within one hour after the goods leave the vendor's facility (whether a vendor-owned facility or a vendor-contracted facility) the customer enterprise should not begin to retain any ship notice information for a maximum of five (business) days before the receipt of the shipment. Retention of the electronic ship notice after the receipt of the shipment is a matter for the customer enterprise to determine: likely several months to one year should suffice to ensure that any chargebacks can be sufficiently researched.

This metric analyzes the vendor's ability to ensure that the electronic ship notice is transmitted sufficiently before the physical delivery of the goods to the customer enterprise's ship-to facility. The customer enterprise must ensure that its own electronic mailbox pickup system and electronic document processing system cycles are short enough, e.g. every 30 to 60 minutes, to account for close-by vendor ship-from facilities that are short trips away from its own ship-to facilities.

METRIC: ADVANCE SHIP NOTICE ACCURACY TO PHYSICAL SHIPMENT

This metric analyzes the accuracy of the electronic ship notice (e.g. the EDI 856—Advance Ship Notice) to the physical shipment delivered. With the exception that damage or theft may have occurred at the hands of the transportation carrier, wrapped pallets and sealed cartons are likely to be trusted with known common carriers. What this metric is focused on is the ability of the vendor to accurately physically ship what is electronically stated on the ship notification in terms of items and quantities of those items.

What is also important is the vendor's ability to accurately pick-and-pack and reflect within the electronic ship notice the item contents (products and quantities) of each carton. In multi-industry vendor compliance in the United States, and this is certainly true in retail, the large barcode on carton and pallet labels, (known as the Serial Shipping Container Code or SSCC), is encoded within the EDI Advance Ship Notice. A customer enterprise, having previously received an EDI ASN from a vendor, would be able to scan a carton (or pallet) SSCC and discern the contents (items and quantities thereof) based on a data match to the EDI ASN. The "shipment accuracy" metric therefore has at least two components: at the aggregate (the entire shipment) level and at the component carton level, with the possibility of the pallet level also as a third interim component if the pallet level hierarchy data segment (data record) is permitted by the customer enterprise in the data mapping, meaning that cartons can be pallet-stacked and not floor-loaded.

Assuming that there are no inaccuracies in the physical receiving process—including the barcode scanning—by the customer enterprise, this metric measures the vendor's ability to properly create the electronic ship notice and accurately pick-and-pack the carton contents. The customer enterprise should select a random sample of cartons from vendor shipments to open and inspect to ensure that the carton contents match the data transmitted in the electronic ship notice. While at the aggregate getting the entire shipment information correct is important, getting what is in each carton identified can be critical from a supply chain standpoint.

METRIC: SHIPMENT PAPERWORK AND LABELING FORMATS; ITEM MARKING AND PREPARATION

This metric focuses on whether shipment paperwork (e.g. the packing list and the bill of lading) and the labels used to mark cartons and pallets conform to the vendor compliance guidelines. Inside the box, another similar metric focuses on whether the item marking (e.g. the store tag with the barcode, description, and price) is accurate and whether the item is shipped properly for immediate presentation known in the U.S. retail industry as being "floor ready."

METRIC: INVOICE TIMELINESS AND ACCURACY

The analysis of invoice timeliness focuses on the delivery of the electronic invoice in comparison to the delivery of the physical shipment. The invoice should not be delivered before the shipment but it should not be delivered too long afterwards. The customer enterprise must specify how long—how many days—after the receipt of the shipment it expects the invoice. This metric analyzes whether the vendor is within or outside the maximum days allotted for invoice delivery.

Aside from invoice timeliness, invoice accuracy is just as if not more important. The invoice should specify which purchase order or purchase orders (if consolidated invoicing is allowed) are being submitted for payment. If backordering is permitted whereby not all of the line items on a purchase order are required to be fulfilled, or if purchase order line items were rejected in a purchase order acknowledgement, then the line numbers on the purchase order may not match the line numbers on the invoice. However, the items on the invoice should certainly match the items on the purchase order along with the prices. If backordering is permitted the invoice quantities may not be an exact match to the purchase order, but this would likely be reconciled by the ERP system upon invoice entry or invoice upload. The ERP system should warn if there is an attempt to process an invoice for an item quantity greater than on the purchase order or greater than a percent variance of the item's purchase order quantity for certain industries that deal in weighed or measured quantities of goods. Duplicate invoice numbers should be checked for and, if received, likely rejected by the customer enterprise, or certainly investigated as to why. One possibility may be a duplicate eB2B transmission error by the vendor.

METRIC: PRODUCT RETURNS AND REPLACEMENTS (A.K.A. QUALITY)

This metric measures the number of different vendor items, and quantity of each item, that are either returned for credit or returned and replaced either for the same item or a similar item, the distinction which should be tracked and, if the replacement is for a similar item, the reason (e.g. the original item is discontinued or the original item is out of stock). The issue of product returns and replacements is one of quality which can be divided into three characteristics:

- Performance: The item does not perform as specified.

- Reliability: The item performs as promised but not for the expected life of the product.

- Safety: The product performs as promised but it is not safe to use. Often this is the case with consumer products that have been determined to be dangerous to children due to having small parts or sharp edges even though the product is not necessarily a children's item.

This metric should analyze the quality of a product, distinguishing the quality characteristics as noted above, in order to ascertain if a pattern is present which may indicate that the vendor is providing defective goods, the product's quality is compromised by use outside of its recommended specifications, or other mitigating factors.

Scorecard Cycle

When it comes to creating the vendor scorecard how often should the vendor be graded: daily, weekly, monthly, quarterly, annually? School report cards provide students their grades at the end of the term (e.g. trimester or semester) for all of their classes at the same time. Each student's classes begin and end on the same date and progress through the school term at the same rate. This is not the case for supply chain data however as I borrow attribute terms from Big Data in that supply chain data moves at varying volume and velocity from one vendor to another. I will also add and explain that supply chain data has the characteristic of vendor confidence which, all together, can play a role into how often a key performance indicator is reported on a scorecard.

Consider for example that a single purchase order initiated by the customer enterprise causes the vendor to create the purchase order acknowledgement, the advance ship notice, and the invoice. Thus the volume of data created by a single purchase order is—from a transactional standpoint—at least triple—excluding the functional acknowledgement documents. (From my experience the amount of data generated per purchase order line item in each of the three aforementioned documents is generally equal to or greater than the data transmitted in the purchase order line itself, depending on the customer trading partner specifications.) Include the routing request and routing instructions, invoice payment remittance and debit/credit adjustment, and the volume of documents generated as the result of just the single purchase order grows even greater.

The volume and velocity of documents (transactions) can be altered based on several different scenarios. The need to acquire the same item can be approached from the following different perspectives:

1.   The customer enterprise can increase the frequency of purchase orders to the vendor, e.g. from once per week to twice per week on different days. This would also increase the volume of purchase orders to the vendor.

2.   The customer enterprise can increase the volume of purchase orders to the vendor, e.g. from one per week to two per week, without increasing the velocity of the purchase orders, e.g. the purchase orders are still transmitted on the same day of the week.

3.   The customer enterprise can retain a consistent volume level and velocity flow of documents with the vendor by increasing the item quantity within the original purchase order.

In all scenarios there will be an increase in the quantity of goods received by the customer because the vendor is shipping more goods, resulting in an increase in the volume of receipt transactions when more pallets and cartons are scanned at the customer ship-to facilities. Different situations may be served by each of the above scenarios independently or combined together.

New vendors will not have had sufficient time in the trading partner relationship to build confidence with the customer enterprise in the vendor's ability to perform in accord with the vendor compliance guidelines. Inasmuch as the monitoring of each metric should be as real-time as possible, new vendors should be graded on a more frequent cycle depending upon each metric and the volume and velocity of the vendor's transactions. If a vendor is only receiving a few purchase orders per month then it would not make sense to grade the vendor on purchase order metrics weekly versus monthly.

As vendors prove their ability to comply with the requirements and their KPI grades maintain high marks, the customer enterprise may decide to extend the cycle of scorecard reporting on certain metrics. Conversely if transaction monitoring reveals that a vendor is faltering too often in a particular area the scorecard cycle should be shortened so that the vendor receives more feedback on their performance. This strategy is in line with my belief of management by exception whereby there is notification only of a problem, both for the customer enterprise and for the vendor.

Not every metric falls into the same cycle (e.g. weekly or monthly) for activity reporting. While every transaction will be monitored for accuracy and timeliness, the aggregate of vendor performance for each metric can be made to be flexible for reporting on different cycles based on volume, velocity, and confidence. This flexible cycle reporting can be used as an aide in helping the vendors to reduce their penalties for non-compliance by improving their performance and increasing their scorecard cycle times to the maximum per metric.

This is not meant to imply that, with robust dashboards and near real-time feedback from supply chain systems, vendors cannot or should not be constantly knowledgeable about their performance on metrics, they should. However what I am trying to differentiate here is that by altering the length of the cycle by metric by vendor based on the customer's confidence in the vendor, the customer enterprise is essentially providing the leeway or breathing room for its well-performing vendors who don't need close monitoring all of the time. As part of a chargeback reduction or forgiveness program for well-performing vendors, metric cycles can be individually extended where vendors have showcased their high marks during the cycle period. Chargebacks are adjusted as long as the vendor's performance for the metric at the end of the cycle remains at or above the current level. Conversely, upon scorecard examination, metric cycles can be contracted where vendor performance slips at the end of the cycle period.

This also lends itself to more of a management by exception initiative for the customer enterprise whereby problematic vendor metrics or new vendors with whom the customer enterprise does not yet have a history of confidence are addressed more often. By allowing the vendors to monitor their performance during the course of the metric cycle and before the scorecard grade is assigned for the metric, the vendor can continually ascertain if their performance during the metric cycle is satisfactorily keeping them out of chargeback trouble. This constant feedback through an online dashboard allows the vendor to self-monitor their performance.

This is analogous to allowing a student to know their assignment, quiz, and exam grades during the course of the term leading up to the end of the term itself. The ability to know how a grade is calculated, calculate a grade-to-date, and project an end-of-term grade is very meaningful for students and vendors alike as the situations are somewhat similar. As I have experience as a university instructor I am well aware how valuable this was to my students who were focused on achieving high grades.

Financial Penalties for Non-Compliance

One of the most sensitive and contentious vendor compliance issues that lies between customer enterprises and their vendors is financial penalties for non-compliance, commonly known as *chargebacks* or to a lesser extent as *expense offsets*. As previously discussed, in the U.S. the Uniform Commercial Code lays the foundation for the buyer of goods to assess financial penalties upon the seller of goods for contractual infractions that negatively impact the merchantability of the goods and opens the door for other incidents that breach the vendor compliance rules and cause supply chain disruptions. These fees can apparently include the costs of administering the management of the penalty itself. The Uniform Commercial Code also provides rights afforded to the seller of goods. In some industries the vendors, either through their lack of knowledge or fear of business loss, do not challenge their customers on the rule of law with regards to their rights, instead being forced to accept their penalties without evidence or recourse. Legal battles are expensive and time-consuming distractions for many businesses to undertake and are simply an impractical way to resolve vendor compliance chargeback disputes. The United States' legal system is based on the presumption of innocence ("innocent until proven guilty"), but too many vendor compliance programs operate in contrast when it comes to the assessment of chargebacks.

As I learned from my corporate governance certification course, (taught through Tulane University's Law School), just because something is legal to do does not make it ethical to do, and doing things ethically means quite simply doing things right. Whatever that "thing" is it just has to be done the right way. But in this case the UCC law seems to be clear that excess penalties by the buyer are not allowed: charging vendors the *cost of the compliance* and not beyond is apparently the limit of the financial penalty.

Chargeback amounts should not be arbitrary: they should be realistic based on the actual infraction and the cost of administering the infraction. I have witnessed chargeback amounts as much as $50 and even $75 for a carton barcode that could not be scanned even when the rest of the label was human-readable. Penalties that assess a fixed amount plus a percentage of the value of the shipment are simply without a basis in reality relative to the actual cost to correct or work around the infraction. The reasoning being made by customer enterprises that come up with these exorbitant financial penalties is that it will lead to more compliance; unfortunately all this does is unfairly and in all likelihood illegally penalize the vendor for a mistake which may—or may not—have been theirs in the first place. Without the evidence it is impossible to know for sure who was really at fault for the infraction, if one really existed at all, whether machine malfunction versus human error at the customer enterprise, or if something occurred at the hands of the customer's designated transportation carrier that the vendor is being assessed the blame.

Chargeback programs should not be run as profit centers—that is not the purpose. The goal of chargebacks is to penalize vendors for their mistakes. But if to err is human, should vendors be penalized for every mistake? Is the customer enterprise, who must act as judge, jury, and executioner in the sole determination of wrong-doing and assessment of financial penalties, so very sure of itself that it can state, without hesitation and without reservation that it is wholly and completely free of error in its ability (computer systems, business processes, and employee skills) to analyze and ascertain for chargeback assignment? I would suggest that this perfect customer enterprise does not exist and as such vendor leeway must be built into the chargeback program.

Customer enterprises can offer to waive chargebacks by metric for vendors who reach a particular and reasonable KPI goal such as 95 percent at the end of a particular metric's cycle period. If the vendor should fall below the KPI goal then either during the next (probably shorter) cycle they are susceptible to chargebacks for non-compliance or they will be billed for the chargebacks accrued during that cycle period. This methodology recognizes that mistakes will happen but does not penalize the vendor for the occasional error. (If the customer enterprise is just beginning its vendor compliance program and adjusting to its own new business processes and systems, setting the no-chargeback goal lower is advisable until such time as trading partners work out the kinks and can move towards more compliance.)

With accurate vendor performance monitoring the vendors who are disruptive to the supply chain will be quickly identified and the customer enterprise will decide whether they represent a commodity product and are easily replaced or provide a unique item and require more involvement to make the relationship work as desired. Establishing unrealistic chargeback programs—goals and financial penalties—makes all vendors suffer, not just those who are purposefully not trying to comply. Ethical actions apply all the way down to the most detailed aspects of an organization's supply chain, yet too many customer enterprises seem to forget that in their corporate mission statements.

There is simply a point of diminishing return where, in the case of a vendor financial penalty, the more severe the less effective at controlling the root cause of the problem, especially when the root cause may not always be the fault of the vendor. Tales I have been told, and in some situations supported by photographic evidence, have ultimately found fault with employees of various customer enterprises from the distribution center to the store, as well as the occasional mishandling by the customer's choice of common carrier.

Before any customer enterprise points the blame solely at their vendors they should consider whether they have provided their vendor community all of the education and toolsets available to be self-supporting and successful in their role as supply chain trading partners. Before assigning excessive fees to financial penalties the customer enterprise must ensure that its own supply chain, including its contractors and employees, are able to act perfectly in their performance each time and all of the time. If not, the customer enterprise is truly the party at fault when a vendor is incorrectly assessed a financial penalty for non-compliance, especially one that is excessive beyond the cost of the correction. No perfect enterprise exists.

Ensure Data Consistency Across Transactions

I have witnessed some egregious examples of poor data consistency across eB2B transactions from customer enterprises—leaders in their respective industries—who, quite frankly, should have known better. In one example a leading office supplies retailer required all EDI Advance Ship Notice transactions to include the pallet-level data segment (data record) even if the shipment was sent via small parcel carrier. I recall that custom software modification cost my client $10,000. And because this requirement was pressed upon all of the office supply retailer's vendors, as opposed to the retailer fixing the internal flaw themselves, the enter vendor community was responsible for bearing the cost of working around the retailer's problem. In another case a department store retailer wanted the store's alphabetic identifier returned on each eB2B invoice but was sending the store's numeric identifier on the purchase order. Again the vendor community was responsible for the customization necessary to address the customer's dysfunctional—and possibly fragmented—software system. A typical U.S. retailer can have from a few thousand to 10,000 vendors, perhaps even more. Therefore for a retailer—or any customer trading partner—to force its vendors to bear the financial burden for its own systematic flaws is wasteful and unfair.

Because the catalyst event that causes a supply chain to come into existence is the need to acquire something, the document transaction most likely initiated by the customer enterprise is the purchase order. Sometimes a forecast transaction is used to provide items, quantities, and dates of release to vendors which allows for long lead-time planning in industries such as electronic components. But from my multi-industry experience it is typically the purchase order that sets the supply chain in motion.

The purchase order—at least in the EDI standard—can vary in terms of how the goods are distributed across destination locations. This is where—at the beginning of the supply chain transaction path—the customer enterprise should examine the data it is sending to its vendor community and determine if it is sending all the data necessary to complete all of the subsequent supply chain transaction documents (e.g. purchase order acknowledgement, advance ship notice, invoice), and whether the nature of the purchase order itself is unnecessarily too complex. If any data that is required to complete a subsequent transaction is missing from the purchase order it should be included. This alleviates the vendor from having to retain unnecessary cross-reference tables, e.g. the numeric to alphabetic store identifiers. Simplifying the purchase order would have likely benefits to those within the customer enterprise who must engage with it—such as the buyer, the distribution center, and the accounts payables areas—because any opportunity to increase efficiency and reduce incidences for error increase throughput and decrease operating costs.

In its perhaps simplest or most straightforward format, an EDI purchase order can be constructed to direct all of the items in the detail section to be sent to a single ship-to location designated at the beginning, or header, of the purchase order. In this scenario the single customer purchase order is translated into a single vendor sales order. This works well for bulk fulfillment orders (e.g. shipments to warehouses) and drop-ship orders (e.g. shipments direct to the consumer).

Instead of declaring the ship-to location in the header, EDI purchase orders can include SDQ (Store Destination Quantity) data segments (data records) as part of the line item detail for each purchase order item. Representing one or many stores and with the ability of including one or many SDQ data segments per line item, a single purchase order detail line representing one item can be designated to have a different quantity sent to the different stores represented in the SDQ segment or segments. (One SDQ data segment can contain multiple pairs of destination locations and quantities.)

Note that because a store identifier appears within the SDQ segment for one item that does not require it to appear within the SDQ segments for the

other items on the purchase order, nor do the same quantities of all items on
the purchase order need to be sent to the same store. For example, the items
on line items 1, 3, 4, and 5 of a five-line purchase order may all be directed to
store 123 but the customer does not desire the item on line 2 of the purchase
order to be directed to store 123; perhaps there is no market for that product
at that store location or there is still sufficient inventory of the item on line 2 of
the purchase order and there is no demand to fulfill yet. The SDQ quantities of
the items on purchase order lines 1, 3, 4, and 5 all shipping to store 123 can be
the same or different as they are calculated based on the customer enterprise's
demand planning system for store location 123.

A single customer purchase order with SDQ segments will represent many
sales orders to the vendor: each sales order will represent one SDQ store with
the ship-to location being either the distribution center that services the store
or the store itself, depending upon the delivery requirements mandated by
the customer enterprise. A purchase order with multiple SDQ locations that
have different ship-to locations—such as different warehouses or distribution
centers—would generate sales orders that ultimately would be separated into
different physical shipments by ship-to location.

All of the sales orders that are the result of the single purchase order
will share the same purchase order identifier: this may cause a replication
problem in the vendor enterprise's ERP system if the purchase order identifier
field is qualified against duplication. Because the customer's purchase order
identifier will have to be retained in its true form on all of the sales orders the
vendor will likely be faced with a software modification to allow the purchase
order identifier to be non-unique or will have to create another data field for
this purpose.

The customer enterprise may limit the scope of the stores represented
on a purchase order with SDQ segments to only stores serviced by a single
distribution center. This helps to narrow the focus of a purchase order for both
the customer and the vendor: both trading partners understand that, while
stores may receive different quantities of different combinations of goods on the
purchase order, the entire purchase order will ship to only a single distribution
center. The SDQ identifier in the purchase order is also known as the *mark-
for store* identifier on the carton label, the same carton label with the Serial
Shipping Container Code represented as the UCC-128 barcode. The mark-for
store identifier enables distribution center staff to direct cartons correctly at
cross-dock facilities.

It may be impractical for customer enterprises to send simplistically formatted purchase orders to vendors due to the complex nature of demand planning and practical need to place a limit on the number of eB2B documents that are transacted. However customer enterprises should examine the data they are sending to their vendor trading partners and ask themselves whether they are truly engaging the vendor community in a way that reduces complexity and reduces costs of data entry and maintenance. Customer enterprises may be surprised to find that in examining this aspect of their business they also may be alleviating some internal confusions and operational overhead along the way.

Don't Twist Terminology

In the first part of the book I highlighted how terminology can be abused when different names can be applied to the same notion: keeping terms and definitions simple will help everyone, customer and vendor employees alike, acclimate to and understand vendor compliance requirements quicker. More egregious than conjuring up new names for commonplace concepts is when a customer enterprise twists the definition of a term, and does so without proper documentation.

Early in my vendor compliance career I was helping a client and we had a sticky situation: we could only fulfill a leading U.S. retailer's purchase order by shipping from both the east coast and west coast warehouses, as neither warehouse had sufficient quantity to fulfill the purchase order in whole. My client could fulfill the purchase order on time, but not from a single storage location. The problem was that, according to the retailer's vendor compliance manual, multiple shipments against a purchase order constituted a backorder and backorders were prohibited, pending financial penalty of course. My client was in a small state of panic and was ready to accept the chargebacks for backorder fulfillment. But there was something that the vendor compliance manual was not stating that made me pick up the telephone and call the retailer's logistics department, and I explained our situation.

Based on my conversation I learned that this particular retailer did not consider an order fulfilled from multiple ship-from locations as a backorder as long as all shipments were delivered to the ship-to location in time. Multiple shipments from the same ship-from location were considered a backorder, but not individual shipments from different ship-from locations. (To be clear: multiple shipments from the same ship-from location, all arriving before the delivery end date, would have been considered a backorder and a chargeback would have been issued. However as long as the multiple shipments did not originate from the same ship-from point, and provided all arrived before the delivery end date, no chargeback penalty would be imposed.) As such, because we were sending one shipment from the east coast and one shipment from the west coast—both before the delivery end date—we were not technically backordering the purchase order. And in the end we received no backorder penalty for our split shipment.

While this retailer's definition of a backorder worked in my client's favor, we would not have known about the skewed definition of what this retailer considered a backorder without my initiative to place a telephone call. Clarity in defining terminology is critical in keeping costs down for non-value-added activities, allowing vendors to get the answers they need from the source documentation provided by the customer enterprise, and promote a vendor compliance program free of trickiness or hidden meanings. Documentation—not telephone calls—gives the vendor community the confidence that they are following the instructions accurately and interpreting vendor compliance mandates correctly. Where a telephone call is required for clarity the customer enterprise should be willing to follow up the explanation with an e-mail to the vendor to state the interpretation in writing in the event the vendor receives a chargeback and requires proof that they contacted someone at the customer enterprise for more information and were following the instructions with which they were provided.

In the end it took two trucks to deliver the total purchase order quantity to the customer. One truck happened to have started its journey from the east coast, the other truck happened to have started its journey from the west coast. Upon arriving at the customer's facility I cannot imagine it made any difference at all from which relative direction each truck began its journey, making me seriously question the logic of this deviant definition.

Keep Compliance Documentation Updated

When vendor compliance documentation is released it should be noted with the date (at least the month and year) of the release. Minor revisions should be recorded in a table of revisions with the revision date, an optional revision number, and a summary of what was revised. The revision identifier (date or number) can be cited in-text throughout the document so the reader knows a change was a revision. This however may get complex as multiple revisions make the content difficult to read due to the continual addition of in-text revision numbers. It would be more practical to only include the most recent revision for in-text citation and retain an archive of previous document revisions. Some customer enterprises highlight (e.g. in yellow) the changes from the previous version. If the tracking of document revisions is too confusing to the vendor community, issuing new document releases using the release month and year as the document's key version identifiers may be the best approach.

Remember to note on the document when the document should go into effect, that is when the prior version of the document is no longer valid for use and when the newer version should be referenced. New versions of some documents will have to be released while the existing document versions are still available as in the case with eB2B specifications and certain operational requirements which may take several weeks or months for the vendor community to implement, thus necessitating the existence of overlapping specifications at any given time. As such not only can documents have an effective date but documents can also have an expiration date.

There are two situations that cause vendor compliance documentation (whether in document, presentation, or web page form) to become dated: it becomes out-of-date or it becomes outdated. When documentation becomes out-of-date the document's expiration date is older than the current date, in other words the document has expired. The document should not be available to the vendor community, or it should be clearly marked as an expired document and its replacement should be clearly identified as the current version. Unfortunately I have seen too many situations where out-of-date documentation is the only documentation available to provide the answers to vendor questions. This cause of vendor frustrations places the vendor in a difficult situation, one where following the only guidance available may lead to chargebacks. Time may be of the essence in getting a shipment out the door, an advance ship notice sent, or a purchase order acknowledgement processed. Having to rely on an out-of-date document leaves the vendor with little confidence in the customer's management of the vendor compliance program and the customer's concern over their vendors and whatever financial penalties may be assessed. It is a bad impression the customer enterprise is making upon its vendor trading partners aside from not being fair in the treatment of their vendors. Out-of-date documents can be available in an archive section of a vendor portal established by the customer enterprise as a courtesy to the vendor community.

Outdated documentation occurs when the documentation has not been updated in a long time. I have witnessed vendor compliance documentation that had not been touched for years that was still—supposedly—relevant per the customer. (The most egregious example is in 2015 while helping a retail vendor client and viewing a customer enterprise's vendor compliance web site with web page copyright years of 2001 and 2003.) Having to rely on documentation that is several years old does not instill great confidence and calls into question the accuracy of the content due to the fact that it is not recent. The solution is rather simple: the customer enterprise should at least update the revision month and year on an annual basis, even if no content is changed, just so the vendor community knows the information was reviewed by someone and it is considered to be current.

Maintaining good document control can be as simple as keeping records in a spreadsheet and a reminder in calendar software. The benefit is not spending non-value-added time fielding vendor inquiries for updated documentation when what is being presented is the most current, even if it has not been changed in several years. Maintaining the confidence of the vendor community only serves to ensure the reputation of the vendor compliance program remains intact and is respected.

Collaboration Beyond Compliance

While not applicable in all supply chain situations, some trading partner relationships mature to the point of such trust between the customer and vendor enterprise that instead of the customer pushing orders to the vendor, the vendor is instead fulfilling product demand in a relationship known as *vendor managed inventory* (VMI). VMI can be applied to raw materials, components, or finished goods (e.g. consumer products).

In VMI the customer enterprise advises the vendor of inventory consumption by sending eB2B documents that advise of product sales or material usage. The vendor will monitor the decline of inventory and fulfill based on pre-established reorder quantities per item or on a calculation based on the rate of consumption across a period of time. The vendor enterprise ships the product and sends an eB2B shipment notification; the customer enterprise receives the product and sends an eB2B receipt notice to the vendor informing of the products and quantities received; the vendor enterprise invoices the customer via eB2B having been notified of the successful shipment receipt. The customer enterprise has likely established a blanket (a.k.a. open) purchase order in advance against which the vendor is authorized to fulfill the inventory and generate invoices.

Vendor managed inventory requires a high level of trust and performance by both trading partners beyond compliance: the vendor may be privy to competitively sensitive information about the customer enterprise's operational and technical strengths and weaknesses in the course of the information shared, and may be able to ascertain certain financial information based on the data. The vendor enterprise is put in a significant position of trust by the customer and must ensure its employees do not use the information being shared for any other purpose beyond the VMI relationship.

Summary

Supply chains—in their software systems, hardware technology, and operations—are complex enough without adding on the burdens of relationship difficulties with the vendor community. Inasmuch as the customer enterprise will be taking the lead role, the customer must also define whether the relationship will be that of combatants or collaborators. A supportive vendor can rescue a customer from a difficult situation, e.g. the failure of a primary supplier or weather-related delays. But this only happens when the supply chain relationship is nurtured and the vendor is engaged enough to want to help when the customer's chips are down.

The customer enterprise should understand the demographics of its vendor community and build a vendor compliance program that its vendor community can acclimate to. Operationally and technically (e.g. software solutions) the vendor community must be able to gravitate to what it is being asked to do and successfully integrate it into their businesses, whether that integration is programmatic or manual, but not such that the vendor must compromise its business in order to do so.

The complex costs of implementing and managing a vendor compliance program can be mitigated if it is conceived and implemented in a methodical manner. The more the non-value-added communications are reduced the lower the costs will be. This is achieved through clear communications, education, engagement, and a continual monitoring and fine tuning of what is and is not working. The cost of a well-run vendor compliance program is less than the expense of the frustrations and non-value-added activities associated with traditional vendor compliance programs and borne by both the customer enterprise and vendor enterprise alike, which only result in the typical animosity that drives a wedge in the trading partner relationship. This is not how supply chain relationships should be defined, as after all the customer and vendor are supposed to be trading "partners."

PART 3

Vendor Education

Introduction

This part of the book serves a dual-purpose: It provides a framework and content for establishing a vendor education program if the reader is a customer enterprise or is a trade association seeking to establish an industry-wide education initiative. It also serves as an educational overview if the reader is a selling company—small or large—looking to take the leap into becoming a more significant player in a particular industry, e.g. retail, grocery, automotive, electronics, pharmaceutical, book publishing, or government. While the industry may be different, the technologies (such as the ubiquitous barcode, the increasing use of radio frequency identification, or transacting business via the use of eB2B) and the methodologies (such as operational excellence in achieving the "perfect order" or recommendations for data integration) really do not vary from one industry to another. It is up to the selling enterprise to embrace excellence in all things that they do that will make them be the successful vendor, the two distinctions in the type of company designation that should be noted as not all companies that sell goods are themselves good vendors.

The vendor education curriculum detailed herein is modeled directly from the supplier education courses that I developed for the U.S. retail industry trade association (VICS) but has been expanded to be generally industry-neutral and applicable to international uses as well and where possible. Retail is a primary economic driver and the U.S. retail industry has been at the forefront of supply chain vendor compliance since my introduction to the topic in 1993.

To start this education I begin with an executive overview of vendor compliance, describing what "vendor compliance" is and how the transition from "selling enterprise" to "vendor" will impact the company. Without executive acceptance to the changes at the selling enterprise the transition will ultimately not be successful, and the trading partner relationship will likely fail in some or all aspects. The trading partner relationship may not get past test status, may not grow beyond or into what the selling enterprise had hoped and invested in, and may result in a poor return on investment if chargebacks are eroding profits or operating miscues are preventing the customer enterprise from having the desire to grow the relationship.

In the second part of the education I delve into detail with regards to organizational recommendations, document management, and recommended standards organizations that provide good sources of information for selling enterprises.

The third part of the education is dedicated to eB2B (using EDI as the examples), including detailed terminology, the pros and cons of in-house versus out-sourced services, information regarding commonly used transactions, and communication methodologies.

The fourth part of the education focuses on the successful printing of barcode labels, with some added information on printing RFID tags. Printing methodology, media types, terminology, and why manufacturers should ensure they acquire a valid manufacturer identifier only from GS1 for their products are discussed.

In the fifth part of the education I will provide eB2B integration tips and tricks, summarizing pointers I have learned from my experiences in mapping and integrating eB2B to ERP systems.

The sixth and final part of the education reviews common chargebacks and how to mitigate or avoid them. Most chargebacks are due to relatively easy-to-correct operational miscues and technology issues that vendors are capable of avoiding altogether.

Executive Overview

One of the first things I tell any selling enterprise considering entering the competitive arena of being a supply chain vendor is that tradition is history: how the company previously did things, technically and operationally, is going to change. The selling enterprise must be willing to embrace new technologies, new business processes, more responsibilities, additional staffing, and employee training and education. Technically the selling enterprise must be able to apply carton or pallet barcode labels, may have to apply RFID tags to cartons or pallets, and may have to barcode or RFID tag items, as well as transact business documents such as purchase orders, invoices, and ship notices electronically via eB2B. Paperwork will still likely be required as with the pack list and bill of lading.

One customer trading partner's requirements will look very similar to—yet will be a little different from—those of another customer trading partner, and these subtle differences, if unnoticed, could cost untold amounts in financial penalties for non-compliance charges. This extends to the format of the pack list, carton and pallet label, and data structure of the eB2B transactions but can also include operational aspects such as whether cartons are "floor-loaded" (no pallet is used) or stacked on a pallet, and the barcode label's position on the carton and pallet. Each customer trading partner's technical and operational nuances must be independently managed yet holistically merged together into the technical and operational flow of the vendor enterprise's systems and processes. This requires leadership, management, investment, and support.

Inasmuch as it is possible to process eB2B transactions successfully without a business software application, the lack of an ERP system will eventually—some people would argue quickly but this timeline is relative—become an unwieldy situation necessitating the need for the selling enterprise to have and house, whether on premise or in the cloud, its business data and the ability to generate meaningful information to analyze and examine its business activity and performance. If the current business software is not capable of eB2B integration then its upgrade or replacement should be strongly considered before the attempted transition to supply chain vendor. I am a big believer in taking small steps to solving problems, and this is not to say that disconnected eB2B and ERP will not be successful … it may only be a short-term solution and the selling enterprise should be aware of the drawbacks of the disconnect.

Aside from the impacts to information technology (notably ERP and eB2B), vendor compliance impacts a company operationally in the following areas:

- *Product Development*: Each unique product or item must be assigned its own Global Trade Identification Number (GTIN), and that GTIN will appear in barcode form on the product's packaging or tag. Product sizes and case quantities may have to be tailored to suit the buyer's desires, and this may vary by customer trading partner for the same base unit product. Preparation guidelines such as "floor-ready" in the U.S. retail industry that dictate hangars and limit fill material may impact existing carton designs or sizes.

- *Order Processing*: The ability—all via eB2B—to receive a purchase order and convert the purchase order into one or many sales orders by ship-to destination (e.g. store or distribution center). Having confidence in the manufacturing and distribution capabilities of the company and inventory accuracy within the ERP system to be able to reply back to the customer enterprise within 24 to 48 business hours with an accurate purchase order acknowledgement.

- *Inventory Management*: Because purchase order lead times will likely be relatively short, the selling enterprise may be required to increase stocks of finished goods in order to compensate for having less time to manufacturer, pick, and prepare. This will also likely mean increasing the quantities on hand of raw materials and components to reduce stock-out situations. Affected items also include shipping supplies such as packing tape, cartons, printer paper and toner, fill material, hangars, and carton labels and ribbons.

- *Manufacturing*: There may be a shift from MTO (Make-To-Order) to MTS (Make-To-Stock) because there is not enough lead time on the purchase order to make the entire order and prepare the order (e.g. pick the goods, pack the cartons, label the cartons, and create the pallets) due to existing constraints (e.g. running one shift, equipment throughput). Making some goods to stock and retaining a reasonable inventory of product may be the only way to mitigate the burden of trying to satisfy order demands within short timeframes utilizing existing capacities.

- *Distribution*: If cartons must be packaged in a certain way, pallets stacked in a particular design, and knowing that each carton must be barcode labeled, the distribution process is likely to take longer than what would be considered normal. Extra time must be allowed for the processing of supply chain trading partner shipments with additional requirements. Pack lists should be verified to case contents before cartons are sealed, and bill of lading documents should be reviewed as a quality check before the shipment is approved for release.

- *Shipping*: Shipment scheduling is a normal function of this process, but the scheduling of shipments for certain supply chain customer trading partners may be more restrictive due to being subject to tighter rules. Consider that customer enterprises will sometimes outsource shipment schedule to a service provider who will likely adhere closely to the rules of their customer: vendors must ensure they allow enough time for their shipments to be scheduled, have their documentation properly prepared upon arrival of the truck, and ensure the shipment is ready when the truck arrives. Gone are the days of delaying a truck due to sloppiness or a lack of preparedness: the truck driver is on a mission and his/her schedule serves a much greater goal.

- *Accounting*: Invoices are no longer sent by paper—they are sent via eB2B. Conversely customer enterprises have and continue to move to paying vendors electronically instead of by check. Invoices may have to be consolidated by ship-to location, e.g. all shipments to stores serviced by a single distribution center, (all individual sales orders split from a single purchase order where the sales order ship-to location is the same distribution center), may have to be consolidated to a single invoice under the distribution center, not individual invoices by store.

- *Human Resources*: New technologies and new responsibilities mean that employee job roles will be changing. Some employees will require new skills training; there may be some new hires required. If processes are not automated some employee work hours may shift. For example, the EDI Advance Ship Notice should be sent within one hour of the shipment leaving the distribution facility (whether that facility is or is not owned by the selling enterprise, e.g. is owned by a contract vendor of the selling enterprise). If the technology employees are responsible for the eB2B processes but their work schedule has them all leave before the shipping department has completed their tasks, the EDI Advance Ship Notice will be late (likely not sent until the next business day) and a non-compliance penalty will likely be assessed for shipments to nearby customer facilities.

- *Operations*: Overall each customer trading partner will have different requirements which must be incorporated into the existing operations processes, yet highlighted and accurately implemented at each appropriate step. Different barcode label formats and pack list formats are likely to exist, as well as different shipment routing instructions and pallet stacking requirements. New costs will be added as new customer trading partner requirements (e.g. an additional barcode label) require not just more materials but also extra labor. How this impacts the cost of goods sold and ultimately profitability is something for the selling enterprise to continually examine as customers are likely to be just as continually demanding that prices remain competitive (translation: the same or discounted).

- *Vendor Management*: If the vendor enterprise has outsourced manufacturing or distribution operations to third-parties, the vendor enterprise may have to establish its own vendor management group to operationally and technically coordinate with its third-parties who may be shipping direct or need to provide more real-time information so the vendor enterprise can respond to its supply chain customer trading partner requests (e.g. the purchase order acknowledgement) accurately and on a timely basis.

The failure to comply with the customer enterprise's vendor compliance requirements will likely result in a financial penalty also known as a *chargeback* or *expense offset*. But the vendor compliance relationship may also include allowances for cooperative marketing expenses and damages, and these contractual allowances (also known as *deductions*) are likely to be withheld from invoices before purchase orders are paid.

A *deduction* is a pre-negotiated amount by the customer and the vendor which represents monies the customer may deduct for business-related expenses, i.e. damages, marketing funds, advertising, etc. A *chargeback* is a pre-defined amount determined by the customer that penalizes the vendor for failures to comply with the vendor compliance rules and guidelines.

The differences between a chargeback and a deduction are significant:

1.   A chargeback is a penalty for doing something wrong; a deduction represents a pre-negotiated or pre-approved expense.

2.   A chargeback should be identified immediately and the root cause addressed to ensure the problem does not perpetuate.

3.   A deduction should be verified immediately, e.g. if a deduction is for cooperative marketing a copy of the advertising should be acquired for verification. If the deduction is for damages a comparison of the damage allowance to the signed vendor compliance contract or agreement should ensure the damages deduction is within the bounds of the relationship; anything above may be an indication of a quality issue and a root cause analysis should be performed immediately. Proof of the damaged goods—such as photographs—should be acquired and an analysis of how the goods got damaged should be performed. Perhaps the product packaging did not permit the item inside to survive a fall from a reasonable height or survive normal handling during the shipment.

Inasmuch as accepting vendor compliance represents an investment it is necessary to take a company to that "next level." But as long as the company is making the investment in technology and operational improvements it should seek to benefit beyond just what is necessary for the customer enterprises demanding it. Because vendor compliance increases the cost of doing business, the investments in technology and operational improvements should be leveraged across the enterprise to help reduce the overall operating costs and drive down the individual costs of goods sold.

For example, barcode labeling and scanning can be leveraged for better inventory control and improved accuracy and throughput during the picking and packing processes. If eB2B is being required with some customers perhaps it can be used with a wider range of customers, even if just to alleviate some of the manual data entry and to automatically import purchase orders into the ERP system with greater efficiency. Implementing eB2B with downstream suppliers—creating vendor compliance requirements—is more of a reality now that the technology and operational improvements are in place in doing so with customer enterprises. The vendor enterprise should consider how it can learn from what it is being mandated to do by its customers with regards to how it can bring efficiencies to its own supply chain operations and relationship with its own vendors. The vendor enterprise should try to offset the expenses with efficiencies via the same investments.

Using the order data collected within the ERP system provides the vendor enterprise with the ability to analyze what items are selling where (geographically) by item attribute, enabling advertising to be targeted better to demographic audiences in a more strategic manner. Perhaps the reason why red and white garments are not selling well in a local area is because the region's university team or football club has as their primary colors blue and yellow; therefore perhaps running local advertisements with garments in the colors of red and white is not a good idea as it is less likely to attract buyers.

There is an opportunity to infuse a new spirit where every customer is treated like they were a "major customer," rather than segmenting out just a few select customers for special treatment. The goals of decreased order processing time and increased accuracy should extend to all customers, not just the largest. On a larger scale this is about showcasing what the vendor enterprise can do and can do very well, versus what its competitors cannot do or cannot do as well. This is where the investments in technology and operational improvements ultimately lead: the capability to out maneuver and out think one's competitor. And it is the vendor who can showcase these skills to buyers who is more likely to win business and grow their business because they are establishing confidence and credibility.

In U.S. retail the ultimate achievement, so to speak, for vendors is the ability to execute the "perfect order" whereby the purchase order is 100 percent fulfilled accurately and on-time, including all barcode labels being able to be scanned, all eB2B transactions being correct and on-time, all cartons being packed correctly, all shipping paperwork being accurate and formatted properly, and all shipments being scheduled and on-time. This ability requires exceptional commitment and capability from the vendor enterprise; it is possible to achieve but impossible to realize without the leadership of executive management.

The Organizational Overhaul

The true essence of what it means to be a great vendor may require—I should say for many companies making the leap "will require"—an overhaul to the organization that must be driven by executive management and embraced by all employees throughout. Executive management must be fully supportive of this endeavor and this includes proper investment in technology, personnel, equipment, and training. There must a single person—a vendor compliance vice president, director, or manager—who coordinates the effort across the supplier enterprise and is empowered by executive management to recommend and/or affect the necessary changes required to maintain compliance with customer requirements. This person acts as a liaison between all departments to translate and disseminate the customer compliance requirements, coordinating activities and scheduling compliance implementations. It is important that each department understands what their responsibilities are and how their roles interact with and affect what other departments are doing, and the vendor compliance leader is the person ensuring this is happening. Representing each operational and technical department, such as those mentioned in the section above, are selected individuals who form a cross-functional team and, with guidance from the vendor compliance leader, ensure their individual departments are keeping to compliance requirements and scheduled changes.

Document management is a necessity and is a must-have organizational trait of the vendor compliance leader. Vendor compliance encompasses various operations and technical documents which must not only be kept up-to-date but also historically retained for version control, my recommendation being at least the most recent 12 months. The ability to review what a customer's requirements were and when they were due to change may help answer the reason for some chargebacks. Some key vendor compliance documents include:

- *Sales Agreement/Contract:* Establishes the relationship between the customer (buyer) and the vendor (seller). Contains information about the products being transacted, including price, turnaround timeframe (from purchase order to delivery), quantity commitments, ship-from locations, deductions for damages, and co-operative marketing expenses.

- *Routing Guide:* Lists the customer enterprise's ship-to locations with ship-to identifier code, location name, and location address. May also include key contacts at each ship-to location. Ship-to locations will typically be distribution centers but may also be retail stores. The routing guide may also contain shipping instructions such as what common carrier to use when shipping within a certain geographic region depending on the shipment type (e.g. small parcel, less-than-truckload, full truckload).

- *eB2B Mapping Guidelines:* Technical information detailing how to interpret inbound data transactions and how to format outbound data transactions.

- *Vendor Compliance Manual:* A general-purpose document that can contain any of the above information plus carton and pallet label specifications, chargeback fees, minimum and maximum carton size and weight specifications, invoicing instructions, key contact information, pack list format, bill of lading format, and general vendor guidelines (e.g. no child labor and no gift-giving policies).

Included with the documents being managed should be copies of the selling enterprise's GS1 manufacturer's identifier certificate, local business license, local tax license, and business insurance certificate. These are examples of commonly-requested proof-of-business documents that customer enterprises routinely require of new vendors, so having them up-to-date and readily available to the vendor compliance lead will save time and trouble in compiling the information for a new vendor package.

Depending upon the industry the vendor is in, vendor compliance may require proof of compliance to security standards such as the Payment Card Industry (www.pcisecuritystandards.org) if healthcare or financial information is being transacted. The vendor compliance leader should coordinate with his or her information technology personnel to gather the appropriate updated documentation necessary related to anti-virus software, hardware and software firewalls, and data security policies. The vendor compliance leader should strive to ensure that all documentation necessary for vendor compliance is readily available and kept up-to-date, not just for its own individual purpose but because prospective customers will be asking for copies of it during a vendor pre-qualification process.

The following web sites should be part of the library of resources that the vendor can reference to help maintain compliance:

- *The customer's vendor compliance web site*: Each customer's vendor compliance web site should be reviewed for changes ideally once per week, at least once every other week. Inasmuch as large enterprises themselves may not be seeking to execute continual changes, their large scale makes them prone to constant changes across their operations and technologies.

- *GS1*: This is the global entity (www.gs1.org) for the assignment of manufacturer identifiers through their country-specific offices such as GS1US (www.gs1us.org) in the United States and GS1UK (www.gs1uk.org) in the United Kingdom. The web site contains useful standards documents such as the proper assignment of global trade identification numbers for products and containers, and an online check digit calculator. With the merger of the U.S. retail industry's trade association, VICS, fully into GS1US, the GS1US web site, under the Apparel/General Merchandise Floor-Ready Merchandise Workgroup contains useful information such as hangar specifications and a color-to-size cross-reference chart. Vendors should rely on the main GS1 web site, their country-specific GS1 web site, and the GS1 country web site of their customers for international supply chain relationships.

- *NMFTA*: The National Motor Freight Traffic Association (www. nmfta.org) is charged with maintaining the SCAC (Standard Carrier Alpha Code) and NFMC (National Motor Freight Classification) identifiers for all North American common carriers. The SCAC is used within the EDI 856 Advance Ship Notice in the U.S. to identify the common carrier; the NFMC is used to identify the commerce being transported.

A list of key contacts, beyond those published, from each customer enterprise by function (e.g. buyer, information technology, accounting, logistics, or vendor management) should be maintained as this information is acquired: customer name, person's name, function or department, telephone number, and e-mail address should be recorded in a master document: a spreadsheet file would do nicely where different tabs were dedicated to a different customer trading partner.

Another web site that would be handy to check would be a weather-tracking web site that enables detailed information focused on the routes taken by the vendor enterprise's trucks or those of its suppliers, contract carriers, or customers. Adverse weather conditions that may impact the function of a customer enterprise's ship-to locations will likely be posted on the customer's trading partner web site. However the vendor should be vigilant about pending declining weather situations and the possibility of having to ship early to beat an advancing storm. The vendor may be required to re-route a shipment to another ship-to location, yet the customer ideally does not want the shipment to arrive later than the original due date. The vendor enterprise must be able to be agile and react to weather-related interruptions even in anticipation of notification from the customer enterprise. Keeping open lines of communication and up-to-date contact lists ensures that when quick decisions are required to be made, the right person can be contacted at the right time. Any delays in the vendor enterprise's down-stream supply chain that could affect their performance in delivering to their customers should be avoided as much as possible, and this includes anticipating weather-related problems.

Vendor compliance cannot be an afterthought: it is something that must be a focus from the beginning because it affects all phases of the pre-sales and sales cycle such as contract negotiation, product development, sales order processing, inventory management, manufacturing, distribution, fulfillment, accounting, and sales analysis. Before a sales contract is signed the vendor compliance requirements must be reviewed and the cost of compliance considered. Can the selling enterprise afford the investment in personnel, advice, technology, inventory, and operations to achieve the "perfect order"? If not then it may not be the right time to consider the transition from selling enterprise to vendor enterprise, and the move may only result in a financial burden due to chargebacks and costs for a one-time trading partner trial. Customer enterprises want to see commitment from their vendors from the first order.

I saw this in the February 2005 edition of *Logistics Today* magazine (now called *Material Handling & Logistics*) and I believe it is just as relevant today as it was in 2005. Called the Customer's Bill of Rights this is what every vendor should aspire to in achieving what is now called the "perfect order" in delivering to its customers the:

- **Right** *Product* in the

- **Right** *Quantity* from the

- **Right** *Source* to the

- **Right** *Destination* in the

- **Right** *Condition* at the

- **Right** *Time* with the

- **Right** *Documentation* for the

- **Right** *Cost*

(To view the article in its entirety, go to: http://mhlnews.com/global-supply-chain/customers-bill-rights)

An Overview of eB2B

Failures in the delivery of and accuracy in supply chain transactions can severely undermine the confidence in the relationship between trading partners. The customer enterprise must take the leadership role in establishing a secure and reliable means of transacting business that also does not prohibit—through the methodology or cost—the supplier enterprise from implementation and continued use. Inasmuch as eB2B solutions do have setup and continuing costs, today the benefits far outweigh the expenses, which have declined with the advent of Internet-based solutions:

- Security: eB2B transactions are very secure to the point where healthcare and financial information is transacted via EDI in the U.S.

- Uniformity: Inasmuch as a customer enterprise will update or modify a transaction format (e.g. a purchase order) on occasion, in between these updates the electronic transaction will always be formatted to the same specifications. Consider that any changes require effort on the part of the customer enterprise too, and affect their business applications as well, so changes will likely be infrequent throughout the year.

- Reliability: eB2B is a highly reliable means of transacting business, more so than postal mail, telephone, fax, or e-mail.

- Integrity: eB2B offers acknowledgement documents for every transaction document sent, confirming at the very least that the trading partner received a document that was transmitted. Further, some transactions such as purchase orders have specific acknowledgement transactions (the purchase order acknowledgement) that exist to confirm the terms and conditions of the original content sent.

- Accuracy: Because eB2B transactions such as purchase orders, invoices, and shipment notifications can be integrated into ERP systems, manual data entry is no longer required, improving accuracy.

- Efficiency: With eB2B-ERP integration capabilities, efficiency increases along with accuracy due to reduced redundant data entry.

Inasmuch as third-party data translation companies are technically not the same as the VANs (value-added networks) whose primary task is to carry the data communications, the difference today is basically indistinguishable and of less importance. Similarly, where once inter-VAN connections—transferring data from one VAN to another—were once unsupported and a likely source of lost transactions, these gaps have been largely closed and this problem rarely if ever the topic of current discussion. What is important to note is that there are achievable (available and affordable) solutions, with services in the marketplace that can aid the customer enterprise in enabling eB2B for its supplier base, from the smallest suppliers using a web-based form to large suppliers transacting and integrating data.

The traditional technical components of an eB2B solution—the communicator and the translator—can be in-house software or an outsourced service. The communicator carries the data from the trading partner's host eB2B system to and from its eB2B electronic mailbox. The translator converts the eB2B data received from a trading partner from the standards format either to a format compatible for integration to an ERP system or for easier readability (e.g. for use in a spreadsheet), or converts output from the ERP system to the trading partners' standards format prior to transmission. Translators can typically convert the eB2B transaction to a basic printout format as well.

The typical eB2B cost structure is one where each trading partner pays for their own side of the communication to and from their electronic mailbox. The cost—usually a monthly fee—may be a combination of a base electronic mailbox fee plus a variable fee based on kilo-characters (every 1,000 characters of data) or the number of purchase order line items. The traditional base mailbox fee plus kilo-character charge been supplanted by more creative and competitive pricing models in recent years though it is still commonly used.

The terminologies used to describe the contents of an EDI eB2B document (file) are as follows:

- Data Element: This is an individual piece of data such as the purchase order identifier. In other references this would be known as a *data field*. A data element is like a word in a sentence.

- Data Segment: This is a single instance of a collection of data elements. In other references this would be known as a *data record*. A data segment is like a sentence comprised of multiple data elements (or "words").

- Element Separator: This is a character that separates one data element from another data element within a data segment, much like a space separates the words of a sentence.

- Segment Terminator: This is a character that signifies the termination of a data segment, much like a period signifies the end of a sentence.

In some cases one data element acts as a qualifier for a successor data element. In EDI, the DTM (Date/Time) Segment in the Purchase Order is an excellent example of the use of qualifier elements as noted in the following examples where the tilde (~) character is the element separator and the asterisk (*) is the segment terminator:

DATA SEGMENT	DESCRIPTION
DTM~001~20081215~~*	In this DTM segment the 001 qualifier informs that the date (in the format YYYYMMDD) is a "cancel after" date, meaning that the purchase order should be cancelled if it cannot be shipped by this date.
DTM~010~20081201~~*	In this DTM segment the 010 qualifier informs that the date (in the format YYYYMMDD) is a "requested ship date," meaning that the customer requests that the order be shipped by this date.

Some data segment types (like the DTM) can occur at various places within a document, in both the header area of the transaction and the detail area of the transaction, and may also occur more than once in the same place (header or detail) with different qualifiers. For example, in the Purchase Order, several DTM segments can exist in the header area to set begin and end ship dates or a delivery date window. The DTM segment (or segment pairs) can also occur for each line item of the Purchase Order to indicate individual line-level ship or delivery scheduling, which may be as an individual date or represented as a pair of dates.

EDI-type documents are wrapped in communication segments known as *envelopes*. Each envelope pair represents a communication start and end segment. The following table describes the envelope segment pairs. If a data translation outsourcing company is used they will (in all likelihood) create all the necessary communication envelopes after they translate the non-standard data to the eB2B standard (e.g. EDI or EDIFACT). Typical information contained in the communication envelope segments includes the sending trading partner's unique identifier, the date and time of the communication, the eB2B standard and version, the recipient's unique identifier, batch counts (e.g. a count of the envelopes or segments) and totals (e.g. the total number of line items). The sequential control numbers used are maintained by each trading partner either in their communicator software or by their outsourced translation and data communication vendor. Remember that these techniques are reminiscent of the time when eB2B was first developed around the 1970s when batch totals and hash counts were widely used methods of ensuring file integrity in mainframe systems. (Speaking from my own experience as someone who began his career as a mainframe programmer, batch totals and hash counts were how we ensured that the files we were to process had integrity as part of our pre-processing routines.) For enterprises which generate the eB2B files themselves and communicate directly with their trading partners, e.g. via FTP, there is likely responsibility to create not only the eB2B-formatted transaction data but also the entire communication envelope at all levels as well, which means maintaining the communication serial number counters control and totaling the end envelope hash counts correctly.

Table 3.1   EDI Envelope Pair Contents

ENVELOPE PAIR	PRIMARY CONTENTS
ISA-IEA (This is the outer-most envelope pair describing the start and end of an entire communication session.)	[ISA] Communication identifiers for the sending and receiving parties [ISA] Date and Time of the document's communication [ISA] Unique communication control number [ISA] Whether the document represents Production or Test data [ISA] EDI standard and version used [IEA] Count of the number of ISA-IEA envelopes [IEA] Transaction control number
GS-GE (This is the mid-level envelope pair, describing the start and end of a group of like transactions such as purchase orders or invoices.)	[GS] The document type, i.e. PO for Purchase Order [GS] Sender and receiver communication identifiers [GS] Document transmission date and time [GS] EDI standard and responsible agency [GE] The number of transactions in the entire group [GE] Group control number
ST-SE (This is the inner-most envelope pair, describing the start and end of an individual transaction, e.g. an individual purchase order, an individual invoice.)	[ST] The document type numerical identifier, e.g. a Purchase Order (PO) is known by its EDI numerical identifier (850) [ST and SE] Transaction set control number, e.g. the purchase order or invoice identifier [SE] The total number of segments, inclusive of the ST and SE segments

The following is a list of common EDI documents and how they are used.

- *Purchase Order*: Used to communicate the commitment to buy goods.

- *Purchase Order Change*: Used to communicate alterations to a previously sent purchase order. This can modify or cancel the designated purchase order.

- *Purchase Order Acknowledgement*: Used by vendors to accept, change, or reject the terms and conditions of a purchase order, including item-level details.

- *Invoice*: Used to request payment for goods that were shipped. (Note: It is better practice to generate invoices from shipments, not from orders.)

- *Payment Remittance*: Used to indicate payment of an invoice. Common use is when invoices are paid electronically (e.g. via Automated Clearing House or Electronic Funds Transfer) without the use of a paper check.

- *Credit / Debit Adjustment*: Used to indicate an offset to an invoice payment.

- *Advance Ship Notice*: Represents attributes (e.g. weight and volume, ship-from and ship-to locations) of a physical shipment of goods including the items and quantities thereof contained in specific cartons.

- *Product Sales Activity*: Sent by customer enterprises, this information typically includes product sales (quantity and monetary values) by store or geography within a date range.

- *Plan / Release*: Sent by customer enterprises to advise their suppliers of interim releases against a blanket or master purchase order.

- *Organizational Relationships*: Established by the customer enterprise to advise its vendors of ship-to locations (e.g. stores and distribution centers) as well as location status (e.g. open or closed) and a status date (the date the status takes affect). The relationship between stores serviced by distribution center is also established in this document.

- *Routing Request*: Used by the vendor enterprise to request routing instructions for a pending shipment of goods.

- *Routing Information*: Used by the customer enterprise to advise a vendor of how to route a pending shipment.

- *Text Message*: Used in the days prior to the development of e-mail when messages and general notifications had to be sent from the customer enterprise to its vendors. Still used as a means of communication because it is basically immune to the common causes of e-mail failures (e.g. spam filtering and full mailboxes).

- *Application Advice*: Typically used to communicate detailed content errors with an EDI document to the trading partner that sent the document. Content problems are related to data not passing the business logic by the recipient trading partner. For example, if a vendor receives a purchase order for items that did not represent products that they sell, an Application Advice could be used to inform the customer of the invalid data content of the purchase order.

- *Functional Acknowledgement*: Used to confirm the receipt of all other (EDI) documents. The Functional Acknowledgement can be used to inform the trading partner that sent the document if the document is syntactically correct, meaning that the document (data elements, data segments, and communication envelopes) meets the eB2B standards requirements.

Barcode Label Printing and RFID Tagging

Customer enterprises must set the requirements not only as to what the barcode labels should look like and how each field on the label is defined (e.g. font size or barcode dimensions, font style or barcode symbology), but also the physical properties of the label itself. The characteristics of the label must consider the environment in which the label is applied and the environment in which the label will live, and these can be two radically different environments. Consider that for some food or blood plasma-based pharmaceutical products, the environment for which the label is applied may be temperate compared to the sub-freezing environment in which the label—and product—is expected to live during storage.

ADHESIVES

Certain adhesives do better in colder environments than others because some adhesives will freeze and crack similar to when water freezes to ice. An adhesive that maintains its cohesive properties in both temperate and sub-freezing temperatures, is corrosive-resistant, or can withstand high-heat temperatures may need to be specified to the vendor community in the compliance documentation along with an explanation as to the various environments the product or carton will encounter.

COATING

There are primarily two coating options: flat and glossy. Flat coatings reflect less light than glossy coatings which reflect more light. In low-light conditions glossy coatings would allow the labels to be more conducive to be read by both humans and barcode scanners. However, in normal and bright-light conditions, glossy coatings can reflect too much light making labels difficult for people to read and, in some situations and depending upon the sensitivity of the barcode scanning equipment, cause so much ambient light reflection that scanner optics could be adversely affected. Most normal situations will call for flat stock coatings but the failure to specify in the vendor compliance guidelines by the customer enterprise could result in inadvertent choices by vendors resulting in disruptions in the customer enterprise's operations when human eyes and scanner optics attempt to read certain vendor labels.

MEDIA

The composition of the barcode labels can range from and include paper, paper-polyester mix, full polyester, and semi-metallic. The media specification is contingent upon the application, e.g. shipping, electronic component identification, outdoor use, corrosive material identification, and is often discussed with the adhesives and the printing methodology especially when ribbons (used in thermal transfer, discussed later in Methodology) are brought into the conversation. The media is important because the labels must survive the application environment, the handling environment (including shipping), and the storage environment, as well as any long-term use for identification marking. The customer enterprise should specify minimum media requirements for general shipping labels and exact requirements where special applications such as outdoor, electronic component, and chemical container labels are produced.

METHODOLOGY

There are two types of print methodology: Direct Thermal and Thermal Transfer. The print heads in barcode printers typically come in 203, 300, 400, and 600 dpi (dots per inch) resolutions. The more dots there are per inch the finer the resolution when printing small characters. This is how dot matrix printers worked but using a series of pins in rows to create characters. Most dot matrix printers were 9-pins though nicer models were 18 or 24 pins. For the most part 203 dpi printers will suffice for standard carton and pallet compliance labels because the smallest font size does not demand the more fine print quality of a 300 dpi print head. However my preference would be to use a 300 dpi print head to ensure increased clarity across all fonts and improved quality when printing barcodes.

With *direct thermal* printing, the print head heats and the heat chemically changes the surface of the media, effectively burning dots wherever the print head elements were heated based on the character to the printed. Thus the white area of the label is where no heat was applied and the black areas of the label—where heat was applied—were burned in patterns based on alphanumeric characters and lines that are human and barcode scanner machine readable. Direct thermal printing does not use a ribbon in between the print head and the media. Because the surface of the media is directly affected by the heat of the print head, it can be also affected by other heat sources such as the touch of human hands and high-temperature environments which will, over time, distort and fade the images on the labels. Inasmuch as direct thermal labels will and do work well in many standard environments for shipping, direct thermal printing is generally not robust enough for extreme environmental situations such as hot and humid warehouses where long-term storage is a requirement and outdoor applications subject to the weather.

With *thermal transfer* printing there is a ribbon that sits in between the print head and the media. The headed print head elements transfer the ribbon material onto the surface of the media, and as such the ribbon material and media pairing must ensure that the combination is a correct match, or else the resultant label will be subject to degradation due to handling and environment. Because of the resiliency that can be achieved with thermal transfer printing and the correct combination of ribbon and media, this methodology is typically used for extreme label environments such as outdoor use and where corrosive materials are handled. Improper ribbon loading can cause a wrinkle-effect across the label and result in printing problems especially when across a barcode making the barcode unable to be scanned. With the right combination of media material such as semi-metallic or polyester, ribbon, and adhesive, thermal transfer applications can resist outdoor, chemical, and tough handling environments.

Setting the print head temperature too high will cause the ribbon to melt and potentially damage the print head; setting the print head temperature too high on direct thermal labels will likely shorten the lifespan of the print head and over-burn the labels. In each print methodology case high print head temperature settings cause a distortion due to a "bleed" of the images, especially around their edges and especially impacting smaller characters and the (narrow) lines of barcodes, making the barcodes less likely to be able to be read accurately by a scanner, especially those on the lower end of the optic scale.

COLOR

In the vast majority of instances the standard white carton and pallet label will be used. However in my experience sometimes a customer enterprise will require labels of a specific color because they act as a visual identifier to the distribution center personnel and allow goods to be handled a little faster. Bright colors—red, orange, yellow, green, and blue—should pose no problem because they will still result in a significant contrast to the black ink or heating from thermal transfer or direct thermal printing and allow sufficient light to be reflected back to the scanner optics. Conversely dark colored backgrounds will be problematic for scanner optics as there is less contrast to the barcode's black bars and less reflected light back for the scanner's optics to read. The customer enterprise should run its own tests in various light conditions and using various scanner optics on the color labels it is considering before integrating them into its supply chain operations and making them a vendor compliance requirement and expense for its vendors. Customer enterprises should also consider whether requiring their vendors to maintain an inventory of multi-colored labels, continually changing in the printer not just to print their labels but to print the regular white compliance labels for each vendors' other customers, is really something to impose upon the trading partner community.

RFID

RFID tags fall into two categories: active and passive. Active tags carry their own power source while passive tags are activated when they are energized by the RFID scanner. The advantage of active tags is that they have a longer field range but the disadvantage is the shorter life span. The advantage of passive tags is their longer life span but the disadvantage is their shorter field range. The challenge in getting RFID into many supply chains such as retail has been the high cost, and the discussion has focused on passive, not active, tags. Because active tags carry their own power source they are more expensive than passive tags.

What is visible on an RFID tag is mostly the antenna configuration, and different RFID tags work within different radio frequencies and therefore might suffer interference from other sources of the same electro-magnetic frequency. For example, a cordless telephone that uses the 900Mhz frequency may interfere with—if in close enough proximity—the scanning of 900Mhz RFID tags, especially while the phone was in use.

Passive RFID tags generally work on the principle of backscatter technology, meaning that the radio signal is sent back to the reader. Problems can occur if the RFID tag is placed on a surface—such as on a carton—immediately backed by a container of liquid or something metallic. Liquids absorb radio frequency signals and metals will deflect radio signals. "Dead air" space should be behind the RFID tag, even if this requires some foam insert or separation barrier.

eB2B Integration Tips and Tricks

Understandably customer enterprises will likely be reluctant to broach the advisory barrier in directing their vendors on eB2B integration to their ERP systems: the customer has no responsibility for how the vendors accomplish this task and cannot bear what will ultimately be the cost burden of fielding questions about this topic. Even offering a general overview or guidance opens the uneasy door for customer enterprises. So it is either left to industry associations—who themselves can provide education and not advisory services—or experts like myself who can provide more detailed information in books and advisory services on consulting assignments.

ERP software typically includes Sales Order Processing, Accounting, Inventory Management, and Distribution (picking and packing) functions. Shipping capability may also exist or may be performed via integration to a third-party product. Of note are the following constraints which vendors should be on the lookout for in their ERP systems when considering eB2B integration:

SALES ORDER PROCESSING CONSTRAINTS:

- The inability to translate an incoming purchase order to one or many sales orders. This functionality may be offered by the eB2B service provider or may be a function of the eB2B software's translation module.

- The inability to validate a purchase order from a business standpoint, e.g. whether the purchase order identifier was already received for the customer, whether the items on the purchase order are all sold by the vendor, whether the quantity for each item is a valid (e.g. some items are only sold in certain quantities and multiples such as 12, 24, or 48), and whether the item prices are valid with current contracted prices.

- The inability to cross-reference GTIN-12 or GTIN-13 item identifiers or the customer's part identifier used on eB2B purchase orders to internal vendor item codes.

- In a retail environment, the inability to establish the necessary location cross-reference information for the customer's stores, e.g. the store identifier, the store's ship-to distribution center, the store's distribution center identifier, the store's corporate parent entity for sales analysis reporting.

- Data field storage requirements possibly beyond the current ERP system's capabilities, e.g. storing the purchase order begin and end ship or delivery date along with the date of the purchase order.

ACCOUNTING CONSTRAINTS:

- Inability to create an outbound invoice from a shipment. (Invoices should not be created from sales orders; invoices should be created from shipments.)

- Inability to consolidate invoices representing multiple sales orders (which were either generated from a single purchase order or from multiple purchase orders) based on same ship-to location. (This gets back to the point that invoices should be generated from shipments and not sales orders; however on some occasions I have encountered ERP systems designed or process flows whereby invoices were generated from sales orders and not shipments.)

DISTRIBUTION CONSTRAINTS:

- The inability to group the pick tickets by ship-to. This will cause inefficiency in operations when it comes to consolidating sales orders as represented by the pick tickets by same ship-to location.

- The inability to create customer-specific carton and pallet barcode labels.

- The inability to create the packing list to the individual customer's layout requirements.

SHIPPING CONSTRAINTS:

- The inability to create the properly formatted bill of lading document.

- The inability to override or establish the correct customer-specific carrier based on the route, shipment type (small package, less-than-truckload, or full truckload) and shipment exceptions (e.g. hazardous materials, jewelry, oversized materials such as canoes or mattresses).

There are several options to overcoming existing ERP software constraints:

1.   Upgrade the existing ERP software.

2.   Modify the existing ERP software.

3.   Purchase new ERP software.

4.   Manually process the eB2B information, likely using an eB2B service providers web forms and separately update the ERP system.

5.   Create external software applications in between the ERP and eB2B systems to bridge any gaps.

How the customer and item data is setup in the ERP system can have a great impact on the ease or difficulty of mapping the eB2B data. What may seem like a logical or routine setup may not be as functional when vendor compliance requirements are suddenly considered.

Who is the customer? Many vendors would answer that the large entity, e.g. "ABC Retailer" is the customer. However in my vendor compliance experience with ERP systems that is not the best data setup perspective. Instead, consider that each ship-to location, store or distribution center, is a customer and the fact that all those customers are owned by ABC Retailer is a characteristic for reporting purposes, whereby another important attribute is the ability to distinguish between a store and a distribution center. Each customer—each Ship To location—can then also have a Bill To location and have a Sold To location such as the corporate parent. The point is that "ABC Retailer" is simply a (sales) reporting attribute; the corporate entity is not a customer that is served in the sense that there are no shipments that will ever go there. It is easier to define a customer or item characteristic field than it is to struggle with hierarchical and feature constraints. "ABC Retailer" is the trading partner; the stores and distribution centers where the shipments are physically sent are the customers.

Items should be established and where possible cross-referenced to each customer's SKU (Stock Keeping Unit) where each item is a defined as being unique by style, color, and size. Each item should have its own GTIN (Global Trade Identification Number), either GTIN-12 (U.S.) or GTIN-13 (Europe). Most likely purchase orders will only use GTIN but may include the SKU and vendor's item number, so the cross-reference capability is a necessity.

Master Data Management (MDM) is the best practice of maintaining good data synchronization—especially applicable to products—between vendors and customers in a supply chain relationship. New product entry dates, current product expiration dates, product packaging carton mixes, and in all instances the related GTINs, should be actively communicated between the vendor and its customers. This is another potential role for the vendor compliance leader, and ideally the data repository would be the ERP system and not an external source such as one or several spreadsheets.

What I am suggesting here—based on my experience—is that the data in ERP systems is typically set up to support sales reporting foremost but that this requires the least effort to support because sales analysis is primarily based on customer, item, and vendor attributes. Therefore, especially when it comes to customer and items, establishing these entities' data structures to support eB2B integration will help alleviate data mapping burdens and will still facilitate, if not enhance, sales analysis reporting. Driving sales reports from the perspective of supply chain relationships is a transition the vendor enterprise should aim to gravitate toward, similar to accepting new supply chain terminology.

With a data setup conducive to supporting eB2B integration, I have found the following methodology useful when integrating eB2B with ERP systems:

1.   Data Unification

2.   Data Validation

3.   Data Supplementation

DATA UNIFICATION

The primary goal of data unification is to drive all inbound and outbound data to a single file format for each type of transaction, e.g. purchase order, invoice, ship notification, without regard to trading partner. This interim data file will meet the transaction requirements across all trading partners and as such some of the data fields may not be used for all trading partners. For example, if creating a unified data file for purchase orders, some customer enterprises may send a do-not-ship-before and a do-not-ship-after date range, while other customer enterprises may send a cancel-if-not-shipped-before date and a cancel-if-not-shipped-after date; still other customer enterprises may send only one date indicating that the purchase order must be shipped by that date. This variety of dates could result in as many as five distinct date fields established in the unified purchase order file, and that is not just okay, that is the point. Once all the eB2B data is decoded from its eB2B standard (e.g. EDI, EDIFACT) and laid out in an easier-to-understand format the mapping to the ERP system is easier to facilitate because the trading partner differences become clearer.

For customer enterprises purchase orders would be exported from the ERP system to a unified data file format before being mapped to the eB2B format and transmitted to the vendors. The various vendors would receive the purchase orders via eB2B communications from various customers and all purchase orders from all customers would be translated into a single unified purchase order file.

The format of the unified data file can—and I would recommend should for simplicity—be *non-normalized* versus the hierarchical nature of EDI and EDIFACT transactions. In non-normalized file structures the header data would repeat for each detail line. For example, in a non-normalized unified purchase order file all the purchase order header information (e.g. trading partner identification, purchase order identifier, ship/delivery dates, ship-to location (if singularly specified in the header), and purchase order date) would be repeated for each detail line. There is no need to create a complex data structure in the unified file, and there is no longer the need to be concerned about saving a little bit of hard drive disk space by not repeating data. The non-normalized file structure makes it very convenient to analyze the unified data in a spreadsheet format because all of the header information accompanies each detail line; in other words each data record is formatted exactly the same. As such line-by-line program processing even becomes more straightforward and there is no question about when the next customer or transaction identifier is encountered.

DATA VALIDATION

Once the inbound or outbound data is driven to a unified file format that file should be used for data validation both before the data is transmitted in the case of outbound documents and before the data is imported in the case of inbound documents. Whether the enterprise is the customer or the vendor ensuring the integrity of the data being sent to trading partners is of the upmost importance to maintain integrity in the supply chain relationship and minimize the chance of supply chain disruptions (and thus incur higher costs) due to bad data. Importing data that lacks integrity or is just incorrect into an ERP (or any) system will only result in problems and cause added costs to be incurred. Two goals of data validation should be to ensure that only good data is sent to the enterprise's trading partners and that only good data enters the business software applications.

Data validation can occur at three levels: individual data fields, related data fields, and against a trusted data source. In my view, dividing the data validation into three distinct processes helps to conquer the different problems individually without creating a single overbearing data validation application that is difficult to maintain. Having three organized programmatic passes per transactional (e.g. purchase order, invoice, ship notice) unified data file that breaks down the different validations may seem objectively no different than one complex audit program, but it is a lot easier to maintain as the validation complexities increase and in some cases become unique by trading partner.

Validating individual data fields is verification as to whether the data field as it stands makes sense. Examples of general rules include item order quantities that should be greater than zero and purchase order ship or cancel dates not earlier than the current date. A quick programmatic scan of the unified data file for obvious individual data field errors can catch what could be critical—and for vendors costly in terms of chargebacks—mistakes before they are transmitted. Similarly customers would realistically not want to send purchase orders with past dates or zero line item quantities, and these audits would service to augment other system checks-and-balances to prevent bad data from leaving the system.

Validating related data fields considers whether certain data field pairs have been created correctly. For example, on purchase orders and invoices, validating that the product of the quantity and the price equal the extended amount may be worthwhile mathematics to perform even though this calculation should already be done within the ERP system, especially if tricky discount policies have spawned complicated program logic burdened with determining the extended amounts. Validating date pairs may be a good idea, just to provide assurance that the dates at the end of the range are always greater than the dates at the beginning of the range, both dates are always valid dates, and the end date is always a set minimum number of (business or calendar) days greater than the starting date if such a minimum criteria exists. If neither date should fall on a non-work day (a Saturday, Sunday, or a day on the enterprise's holiday calendar), this validation can be performed against the unified data file before mapping for outbound transmission to vendors.

In the unified data file field qualifiers used in the eB2B transaction may be a part of what is included. For example, as is typical on purchase order and invoice line items, the GTIN-12 which is formerly known as the UPC (Universal Product Code) and is often qualified in a preceding data element with "UP" to signify that the subsequent data element identifier is a GTIN-12 (UPC). Likewise the GTIN-13 which is formerly known as the EAN (European Article Number) is often qualified in a preceding data element with "EN" to signify that the subsequent data element identifier is a GTIN-13 (EAN). Knowing that the GTIN-12 is always 12-digits in length and the GTIN-13 is always 13-digits in length, a data validation between these two related fields would ensure that "UP" is always the qualifier for GTIN-12s and "EN" is always the qualifier for GTIN-13s. This would also be true if a company was involved in the sale of books where the ISBN (International Standard Book Number) qualifier in eB2B transactions is typically "IB." Assigning the wrong data qualifier to a data element can make the eB2B document unusable by the trading partner and, for vendors, may result in chargebacks.

In the prior two levels of data validation, the data to be validated was basically isolated to itself, contained within the unified data file. The third level of data validation is to compare the contents of the unified data file against a trusted data source. In the example of a unified data file of purchase orders, ensuring all of the line item products are those that belong to the vendor before the vendor enterprise attempts to import the file would be a wise review: I have experienced customer trading partners who do occasionally send purchase orders with items that do not belong to my vendor clients. A comparison of the translated unified file to the item master is a relatively easy verification to perform. If the vendor enterprise requires some items to be ordered in specific quantities or quantity multiples (e.g. 12, 24, 36, or 48), validating the unified data file for those products and auditing the quantities would be recommended before importing the file of purchase orders as sales orders into the ERP system. This is predicated upon what level of business rules the ERP system has in its own ability to validate inbound data; if the ERP system is not capable of this level of business rule logic then an external audit of all eB2B data before attempting an import into the ERP system is recommended. Audit errors can be identified and the questionable transactions held while the transactions that pass the checks are allowed to be imported into the ERP system.

I recommend an "all-or-none" approach whereby if any part of the header data or any line item on a transaction is in question the entire transaction is held in suspense until resolved; only if all data on the header and in the line items on a transaction pass the audit checks will the entire transaction be allowed for import.

Inbound purchase orders and inbound invoices can be checked against the enterprise's ERP or accounting system to determine if the transaction identifier (the purchase order identifier or the invoice number) already exists for the particular trading partner. If so, is the trading partner sending a replacement or is the trading partner sending a duplicate in error? Instead of importing questionable data into the enterprise's business software application it would be best to hold the transaction in question in suspense until the nature of the duplication is determined. Remember: just because a duplicate is found to exist does not mean that all ERP systems will prevent it from existing; not all purchase order identifier data fields on the sales order header in all ERP systems are established as key fields where the contents must be unique. Further, the uniqueness of the purchase order identifier field on the sales order header may be a configuration setting in the ERP system setup. The invoice identifier is likely a unique field and a duplicate identifier will likely be prevented from existing, but this may be a software-dependent feature and as such can vary from application to application.

Some eB2B transactions may be marked as a replacement of a previously sent transaction of the same identifier. If this is the case then the enterprise must ensure the previously sent transaction is properly cancelled, not just deleted, from its business software before the replacement transaction is imported or else a replicated (though not exactly duplicated) transaction will simultaneously exist. Because a human will likely have to be involved in the decision as to whether a duplicate transaction identifier is a replacement or an error and then affecting the business process in the handling of each situation, holding out the questionable transactions apart from the business software application until they are resolved is a wise move. My general advice is: "When in doubt, keep it out."

DATA SUPPLEMENTATION

Not all ERP systems will be able to hold all of the eB2B data demanded by trading partners. This will be a particular struggle for vendor enterprises in trying to comply with the requirements of multiple customers. Item cross-references to customer SKUs (Stock Keeping Units) or part numbers, store and distribution center relationships as well as addresses and identifiers, item pricing (which may become customer-specific and can result in customer-specific item identifiers), gift messages, and item configurations (e.g. different packaging quantities by customer) are examples of data setups which some ERP systems may be unable to support.

One option is to modify the ERP system and add the necessary data fields to existing data tables. The advantage of this option is that the data is retained together and within the ERP system. The potential disadvantage is the cost of customization and the impact on accepting new upgrade releases of the ERP software: some invasive customizations may prevent the software from being upgraded to new releases, at least easily and without incurring additional customization costs each time.

Another option is to create completely separate external data tables that act to supplement the ERP system's existing data tables. Using the same data table key values (e.g. purchase order identifier, invoice number, item identifier, sales order number) these supplemental data tables exist solely to store the additional transactional data the ERP system's native data tables cannot. The idea is that the supplemental data tables would be used to amend and append data to any outgoing documents beyond that which could be stored in the ERP system, and that this is performed programmatically outside the ERP system. In addition the ERP system would reference these supplemental data tables as-needed for any internal processing, e.g. to include a gift message on a special packaging insert or on a carton label. However instead of modifying the structure of the ERP system's native data tables, the use of external supplemental data tables provides more flexibility without the typical negative consequences associated with invasive customizations. Inasmuch as program code will have to be changed at least the base data table structures will remain intact. And given that these supplemental data tables are more likely prone to frequent change maintaining them outside the ERP system may provide the best balance of flexibility without significant maintenance downtime.

Avoiding Common Compliance Chargebacks

Some of the most common—and costly—vendor compliance chargebacks are also typically the most simple to avoid, requiring modest investments in technology and a dedication to operating in an organized manner. Supply chains primarily rely on technologies that are decades old—eB2B and barcodes—even if the communication methods and scanning science has evolved. Similarly the basic business processes have been established a long time ago and have been proven to work well; modern technologies have made them work more efficiently and have provided more throughput but the basics of processes such as order picking and packing have remained consistent over the years. I mention all of this because correcting the problems that cause so much supply chain disruption simply require getting down to the basics.

It would service this topic well to begin with a clarification of what types of expenses can be withheld from invoice payments. As previously noted, "chargebacks" are financial penalties for failing to comply with vendor compliance requirements. The Uniform Commercial Code in the U.S. refers to damages due the customer enterprise from a vendor's failure to comply with terms of the buyer-seller relationship as "deductions." However in traditional supply chain terminology there is a difference between "chargebacks" (also known as "expense offsets") and "deductions." Where a chargeback is a financial penalty for non-compliance, a deduction is a debit to a vendor invoice because the customer is taking an allowed compensation for a pre-negotiated expense. Examples of pre-negotiated expenses, which should be noted in the customer-vendor accord, are co-operative marketing dollars and damage allowances.

Understanding the difference between a chargeback and a deduction is the first step to problem identification and resolution. Sometimes the vendor's Accounts Receivable department will be the first entity to be aware of a chargeback because they will notice the debit from the invoice payment remittance and amount difference. Chargebacks and deductions should be recorded differently on the company general ledger so they can be tracked separately. The failure of the Accounts Receivable department to distinguish chargebacks from deductions and types of each can lead to incorrect calculations for cost of goods sold, actual marketing dollars spent, damage allowances, and chargeback write-offs.

For each chargeback the Accounts Receivable department receives it should either notify the Vendor Compliance leader or, if no vendor compliance leader is present, attempt to analyze the base nature of the chargeback (e.g. technical versus operational) and direct the information to a dedicated person within the technical and operational areas of the company.

Having disseminated the chargeback information, a root-cause analysis should be performed. Information such as the chargeback date, chargeback amount, trading partner, chargeback problem type, and document identifiers (e.g. customer purchase order identifier, vendor pick list identifier, vendor invoice number) should all be recorded in a spreadsheet or simple database for case management. When the cause of the chargeback is determined, this information should be entered and the case closed. Chargeback investigations are not a blame game or witch hunt but they are a determination as to the source of the problem: personnel, training, equipment, operations process, or technology. (In fact these would make for good chargeback classifications for analysis reporting.)

Sources of information for chargeback analysis can be found in the company's ERP system, the eB2B system, documentation (e.g. pick lists, packing lists, bills of lading, invoices, purchase orders, sales orders, vendor compliance documentation), e-mails, barcode labeling applications, and any custom software applications that are used within the supply chain business processes.

BARCODE LABEL PLACEMENT

Misplaced barcode labels on pallets and—especially—cartons are a common source of chargebacks. This problem is easily corrected by having score marks printed on the shipping cartons. These score marks should be guides directing the placement of the barcode label at each corner of the label.

When stacking labeled cartons on a pallet, typical vendor compliance guidelines will require all labels facing in one direction. This reduces the need for the receivers to have to spend the time turning the cartons to find the side with the barcode labels before placing the cartons on the conveyor belt for automated scanning or taking the time and energy to handle the cartons when manually scanning the barcode labels. In large-scale operations wasted seconds add up to wasted minutes and ultimately result in wasted hours, so every movement that does not add value is eliminated.

BARCODE LABELS NOT READABLE

If a barcode cannot be read when it is scanned the problem could be one of several possibilities:

- The label has a wrinkle in it going through the barcode. This could have occurred when the label was being affixed to the carton. Taking better care during the manual handling of the label will resolve this. If automation is used to affix the barcode labels the machine should be checked and will likely need maintenance.

- A wrinkle through the barcode could also be the result of the ribbon used in thermal transfer printing not being installed correctly. Ensure that the ribbon is aligned correctly while installed in the printer.

- The barcode printer print head temperature may not be set correctly. If the print head temperature setting is too high the print head will cause a bleeding effect, blurring the lines of the barcode into the white areas and rendering the barcode unreadable. If the print head temperature setting is too low there will not be enough heat to alter the direct thermal coating or transfer the ribbon ink, in either case the result causing sketchy, broken, and light barcode lines which will be insufficient to be read reliably.

- Inasmuch as labels can be printed on standard office ink jet and laser printers, these methods and media are not known for being as resilient to the rigors of the shipping and handling process versus thermal printing methodologies: the labels may simply not be rugged enough to survive the journey, especially in hot and humid environmental conditions.

- Barcode printer head elements can fail, and the failure of some of the "dots per inch" can compromise the integrity of a barcode. Ensure barcode print heads are cleaned and maintained and changed when they are at the end of their usable life expectancy.

LATE ADVANCE SHIP NOTICE

From my participation on the then U.S. retail industry association's committee, the consensus for the maximum amount of time between the ground transportation carrier leaving the distribution center and the eB2B advance ship notice transaction (e.g. the EDI 856—Advance Ship Notice) being sent is one hour. This can be a problem for many vendors because it relies on technical support after the last truck has left, and typically the information technology staff has themselves already left for the day leaving only the distribution center personnel to finish up and get the last shipments out the door. The problem is compounded when the customer's receiving facility is geographically close by and the advance ship notice cannot be transmitted until the following business day because the shipment will have already arrived at the customer's location.

This also applies to—and is further complicated by—shipments from subcontractors of the vendor. The advance ship notice must have all the identity markings of having come from the customer enterprise's vendor, not from a subcontractor of the vendor because that is irrelevant to the customer. Therefore either the vendor enterprise's subcontractor must have the capability to send an advance ship notice on behalf of its customer (the vendor) or transmit its shipment information to the vendor enterprise for turnaround to the customer enterprise within one hour.

The only solutions to this problem are to establish a fully-automated system or to make sure technology staff is fully engaged to support the operations staff and subcontractors as-needed. This is one—probably the one—area of chargebacks that is not able to be solved easily due to the aggressive tight timeliness of the advance ship notice transaction sent in relation to the departure of the shipment, as well as the necessity of close coordination with vendor subcontractors to deliver accurate information on time.

WRONG SHIP-TO ADDRESS

Vendors are required to keep up-to-date with their customer's ship-to locations, including the stores serviced by distribution centers in the case of retail. Locations may geographically move but retain the same identifier. Adverse weather conditions (e.g. snow storms, floods, hurricanes) may necessitate a customer enterprise to reroute shipments from one distribution center to another. Vendors are responsible for keeping up-to-date with their customer's organizational relationships but should also be aware of potential weather conditions that could possibly cause a temporary alternate route to be put into effect. And because the alternate route may take longer transport time the vendor enterprise may need to expedite manufacturing, picking and packing, shipment preparation, and shipment scheduling in order to meet the same delivery schedule date.

PACK LIST PROBLEMS

If the pack list is missing from the carton the cause is likely procedural in the vendor enterprise's distribution center operations. Employee training is likely required to ensure that each carton—or the lead carton as appropriate—contains the pack list. The pack list must be an accurate reflection of what is being shipped in both the items and the quantity of items: there must be no deviation between the data on the documentation and the contents of the carton. For vendor enterprises, using barcode scanning against the sales order and verifying the pick-and-pack process will help to reduce errors.

If the pack list is not formatted according to the customer enterprise's specifications this is a software issue to be resolved within the ERP or distribution application. The format of pack lists may differ, even if slightly, between customer trading partners. Sometimes customer enterprises will yield on their pack list specification if the vendor presents one that is very close; customer enterprises are generally aware of the burden vendor trading partners face in trying to comply with the myriad mix of multitude customer requirements and some are more sympathetic than others. Nonetheless, ensuring the right formatted pack list is printed for the assigned customer enterprise is the burden of the vendor.

INCORRECT CARTON COUNT / MISSING CARTONS

A problem prone to large orders, missing cartons is typically the result of poor procedures and a lack of control in the distribution facility. This can be remedied by improving operational procedures that include dedicated areas to shipment preparation and better control over carton counts. Using the UCC-128 barcodes found on standard compliance labels, the scanning of these barcodes and comparing to the contents of the advance ship notice is one method of verifying that all cartons are accounted for. Creating separate carton count labels with unique identifier barcodes and placing them on a different carton side than the UCC-128 label for scanning and reconciliation is another option though the additional label cost and labor to affix the label is a consideration.

MISSING ITEMS OR INCORRECT ITEM QUANTITIES

The errors leading to pick and pack the incorrect items to fulfill an order, the inability to ensure the full quantity of ordered items were selected, or failure to pick and pack all of the items the customer ordered to fulfill an order are all likely related to poor operations practices and a lack of technology tools and operational procedures to ensure sufficient checks-and-balances are in place.

Poor warehouse management that results in items not being in their correct inventory shelf or bin location will hamper order fulfillment accuracy. The problem can be compounded by look-alike items such as machined parts (e.g. bolts, screws, washers, gears, mechanisms) or consumer products that may look similar but differ in material, size, function, picture or some other means not easily noticeable to humans, especially those who are conflicted by low wages and under pressure to get a job done quickly.

The use of auto-identification technology—most notably barcode labeling and scanning—can readily reduce the rate of these errors significantly. By scanning item barcodes and comparing the scanned data to the line item data on the order it is possible to warn against picking the wrong item, over picking the right item, and alert when not enough of a correct item has been picked at the end of the picking process. Other technologies such as pick-to-light direct picking personnel to the bins where the inventory is located and identify the quantity required to fulfill the order. Separating the picking and packing processes permits a check-and-balance audit whereby the pack process verifies the pick process in terms of both item and quantity accuracies against the order.

Insufficient inventory due to out-of-stock situations which result in backorders is a different issue. This is resolved through analysis of raw material or finished goods purchases and lead times, manufacturing scheduling and throughput, customer consumption (sales order analysis), and replenishment settings (e.g. minimum on-hand quantity, maximum on-hand quantity, re-order quantity) in the ERP system. I am certain that there are plentiful books on this topic. Within the confines of successful vendor compliance, with inventory available, the vendor's inability to successfully fulfill an order is likely due to a lack of good operations practices and the necessary technology tools.

PRODUCT PACKAGING AND PRESENTATION

U.S. retailers have been demanding a reduction to the amount of packaging fill material used by vendors having recognized the cost of storage and disposal upon their operations. Green initiatives are seeking to replace the traditional foam packaging materials with inflatable airbags and recycled paper. Vendors who cannot conform to these new initiatives can face financial penalties for non-compliance.

The shipping cartons must be strong enough to withstand the journey from the vendor enterprise's ship-from location to the final destination. This directly impacts the damages allowance typical in U.S. retail vendor compliance agreements: a percentage the retailer is entitled to deduct for product damages.

The vendor should not give the customer any (additional) excuses to take damages deductions beyond those that are actually occurring.

Cartons of sufficient strength, properly sealed with strong tape, and using the right inner packing to protect items against damage will help to reduce damages that could lead to product returns—an operational cost both the customer enterprise and the vendor enterprise should be seeking to avoid—and damage deductions for the vendor. A hint to customer enterprises: colored packing tape is an effective visual indicator that can be used to denote packages for specific routing or contents (e.g. red packaging tape means perishable goods). But my warnings persist: While this sounds like a clever idea, is this something reasonable to ask your vendors to do?

EB2B ERRORS

Errors related to eB2B issues are typically those that are the result of improper document formatting or timing issues. Improperly formatted documents—documents not meeting the customer enterprise's specifications—are likely due to the vendor enterprise's failure to keep up with the eB2B changes by their customer trading partners. This is certainly a challenge especially if the vendor enterprise is responsible for the eB2B translation mapping in-house versus using an experienced outsourced third-party service provider. Nonetheless, even if the vendor enterprise is using a third-party service provider for eB2B data translation and communications, eB2B-to-ERP mapping may be presenting some challenges that leave the vendor enterprise incapable of complying with the customer trading partner's requirements. For example if the customer trading partner decides to send a begin and end ship date window with each purchase order but the vendor enterprise's ERP system does not have the additional data fields at-the-ready to store the additional begin ship date and end ship date for the sales order. The vendor may be shipping or delivering too early or too late because of a lack of capturing and processing the date pair.

The timeliness of response documents presents another area of concern and potential financial penalty for vendor enterprises. The purchase order acknowledgement is typically required to be turned around within 24 hours from the receipt of the purchase order. If the turnaround time is 24 business hours the vendor enterprise has some leeway, e.g. for purchase orders received on a Friday. If the turnaround time is 24 clock hours, this can be a problem for vendors without automated systems who receive purchase orders on Fridays and would have to wait until Monday to turnaround a purchase order acknowledgement. Purposefully not receiving purchase orders until the upcoming Monday is one possible solution, however this does reduce the amount of reaction time the vendor has to action the purchase order. The vendor may still receive a chargeback if the expectation of the customer enterprise is that purchase orders must not sit idle in the electronic mailbox for more than 24 hours without being acknowledged, as this would be flagged as an exception.

The ability of the vendor enterprise to turn around or respond with eB2B documents on such a timely basis, and with the help of their own vendor community, is in and of itself a supply chain challenge to manage, requiring a commitment to operations excellence and an investment in eB2B technologies, some of which may have to run on an automated schedule and interact freely (without human intervention) with the ERP system.

A CHECKLIST OF PROACTIVE STEPS TO REDUCE CHARGEBACKS

In summary, here is a checklist that vendor enterprises can do to reduce the incidences of financial penalties for non-compliance to their customer trading partner's supply chain vendor compliance requirements:

1. Keep up-to-date with the customer enterprise's operations, logistics, and eB2B requirements by regularly (e.g. weekly) checking the customer trading partner's vendor compliance web site.

2. Vendor enterprises should educate their personnel to be on the lookout for problems that can cause chargebacks. These problems should be reported to a lead person who is authorized to take the steps necessary to affect operational and technical changes to minimize the reoccurrence of the problem. This lead person will document the problem from source to solution.

3. Vendor enterprises should train Accounts Receivables staff to catch and report chargebacks right away, and to understand the difference between a financial penalty for non-compliance and a pre-negotiated deduction.

4. Invest in technology—such as barcode printers—to ensure high quality barcode label output. Make sure the right selection of adhesive, media (flat versus glossy, paper versus paper-polyester, full polyester, etc.), and method (direct thermal versus thermal transfer) is researched and chosen.

5.   Invest in technology — such as barcode scanning — to ensure accurate carton counts and item selection during picking and packing.

6.   Create and follow a preventative maintenance schedule for printers producing barcode labels.

7.   Ensure all product packaging is sufficient to allow products to be shipped undamaged and floor-ready. Use only compliant fill materials and cartons strong enough to withstand the journey and protect the contents.

8.   Use good procedures to ensure all paperwork is properly generated and is sent along with the shipment.

9.   Make sure that response or turnaround eB2B documents are sent within the necessary timeframe parameters.

Obtaining a Proper Manufacturer Identifier

In 2005 the Uniform Code Council, which assigned manufacturer identifiers for North America, and the European Article Numbering Association, which assigned manufacturer identifiers for Europe, merged into the global organization known today as GS1. Manufacturer identifiers are a key component of the Global Trade Identification Number (GTIN) system, such as the GTIN-12 (the 12-digit identifier formerly known as the UPC or Uniform Product Code) and the GTIN-13 (the 13-digit identifier formerly known as the EAN or European Article Number). Other GTINs include the GTIN-14 which is used to identify a carton of multiples of a single GTIN-12 or GTIN-13. The 18-digit Serial Shipping Container Code (SSCC-18) barcode (the two prefix digits are not counted when referencing this barcode) used on carton and pallet labels and which is included in the EDI 856 Advance Ship Notice document contains the manufacturer identifier as well. And the GS1 manufacturer identifier is used in the GS1 Global Location Number (GLN), an identifier for ship-from locations.

GS1US has a guide titled "GS1 Healthcare US—Implementation Guideline" that provides information on the relationship between the U.S. Food and Drug Administration's National Drug Code (NDC) and the GTIN structure of GS1. Briefly, the 10-digit NDC is composed of two pieces of information: a labeler code and a product/package code. GS1US has reserved the prefix placeholder "03" for use with NDCs. This is why all pharmaceutical products in the United States have a prefix of "3" on their product GTIN-12 (UPC) barcodes, as the "03" is reduced to just the "3" and the addition of the 10-digit NDC with the check digit results in the 12-digit GTIN-12 / UPC.

Traditionally in the United States (and for North America) the Uniform Code Council was the sole-source for a manufacturer identifier. But the advent of the Internet has brought forth independent companies that advertise for sale blocks of barcode numbers (either GTIN-12 or GTIN-13) based on a manufacturer identifier. The prices are more competitive—lower—than purchasing a manufacturer identifier from GS1. So, is this okay or does it open up the possibility for supply chain disruptions? What is the position of GS1 on this topic?

Let me start with the answer: Manufacturer identifiers should only be acquired from GS1[1] and not from any other source, including and especially an independent company who is—and who typically is—a reseller of barcode label software, hardware, and consumables (the ribbons and labels) or services. In a conversation on this subject with a representative from GS1's United States office back in 2009 I was informed that GS1 was aware that this practice—the independent sale of blocks of barcode identifiers—was occurring, but that GS1 is a standards organization and not a policing agency and there was nothing GS1 was able, or was willing, to do about this. I am in disagreement because, while granted nothing illegal is happening, GS1 does have the ability to qualify who purchases a manufacturer identifier and can set the standards for what a purchaser does with their manufacturer identifier and the ramifications for breaking the rules, such as revocation of the GS1 manufacturer identifier, thereby leading to and including legal action. The importance of the GS1 manufacturer identifier has impacts to global data synchronization and smooth supply chain operations and therefore should not be taken lightly by the sole organization in charge of its keeping and assignment. So why is the manufacturer identifier

---

1   Or the appropriate regulatory body or government agency, as in the case of the U.S. FDA for pharmaceuticals in the assignment of the labeler identifier.

so important, how it is used in the supply chain, what exactly is going on, and where do the problems lie?

The manufacturer identifier—now known as the GS1 Company Prefix—is a unique number that is assigned to the manufacturer of a consumer product. Traditionally in North America the manufacturer identifier was six digits in length. Due to the sheer increase in the volume of manufacturers requesting a Company Prefix the numbering system had to be changed to be more flexible. Now the GS1 Company Prefix can be either 6, 7, 8, 9, or 10 digits in length, but this comes at something of a cost: The longer the length of the Company Prefix, the fewer the number of concurrent unique product identifiers is possible. This is because the GTINs, e.g. the GTIN-12, is of a fixed length (12 digits). With one digit reserved for the check digit, (the right-most digit in many barcodes is the calculated check digit such as in a GTIN-12, GTIN-13, GTIN-8, GTIN-14, and UCC-18), leaving 11 digits remaining in a GTIN-12, the more digits in the Company Prefix the fewer digits in length for the *item reference number*, the remaining digits to be used by the manufacturer. The item reference number is simply a serialized number assigned by the manufacturer to a unique product. For example, if the Company Prefix is 0123456, the first item reference number should be 0000, the next item reference number should be 0001, followed by 0002, etc. If the Company Prefix is 123456789 then the item reference number range is limited from 00 to 99 because it is restricted to two digits in length, thus allowing only 100 concurrent unique items.

Trying to assign intelligence to the item reference number with regards to the products they represent is, from my experience, a losing proposition, and I have long advised my clients against doing so. It is simply best to start at the beginning with the first product identifier assigned to the zero item reference number and, simply and sequentially, reference the products.

A spreadsheet is a very effective means of keeping this list so the next item reference number to be assigned is readily available, especially if the ERP system is not able to sufficiently store the necessary data. Key data to track in spreadsheet columns should include:

- The manufacturer's internal product identifier.

- The product description.

- The GS1 manufacturer identifier.

- The manufacturer-assigned GTIN item serial number.

- The calculated check digit. (This calculation can be embedded in the spreadsheet using the characters in the GS1 manufacturer identifier and the GTIN item serial number, or the check digit calculator on the GS1US web site can be used and the result entered.)

- Product availability date.

- Product termination date.

An item reference number is assigned to a unique consumer product typically differentiated by any alteration to style, color, or size. Product packaging can be a style differentiator: the same 100 percent pure orange juice in a 64 ounce glass container versus a 64 ounce plastic container would have two different item reference numbers. Each item reference number is related to a unique GTIN.

The GS1US web site—www.gs1us.org—provides guidance on how to select a Company Prefix based on the anticipated number of concurrent unique products the manufacturer will have at any given time. And per the GS1UK (United Kingdom) web site—www.gs1uk.org—companies that run out of item reference numbers series can apply for an additional global company prefix at a reduced rate. The general guideline is that an item reference number can be reused after it is dormant for at least 48 months, (30 months for clothing, 12 months if the product never actually went to market), as to allow all trading partners involved to flush their inventories of the discontinued product. (Thus the importance of tracking the product's availability and termination dates.) Note that GTINs assigned to Regulated Healthcare Trade Items are prohibited from ever being reissued.

When a manufacturer identifier (Company Prefix) is purchased from GS1 that identifier is wholly and solely for use by the purchasing company. All of the item reference numbers within the allowable range based on the number of digits in the item reference number (which we now know is a factor of the length of the Company Prefix) belong to the purchasing company. This is not necessarily the case when "blocks of barcodes" are purchased from independent resellers who have likely purchased a Company Prefix from GS1 in the low number of digit range (e.g. six digits) and are looking to sell off groups of item reference numbers the same way one might divvy up a parcel of land into smaller sections.

If an independent reseller of "blocks of barcodes" owns the Company Prefix 0123456 this means that item reference numbers 0000 through 9999 are available. The independent reseller could subdivide the 10,000 item reference numbers available into many small packages of 10 or 25, allowing for multiple manufacturers to purchase one or several series of item reference numbers belonging to Company Prefix 0123456. The end result is that multiple manufacturers would be using the same GS1 Company Prefix (e.g. 0123456) though none of these manufacturers would actually be assigned true ownership of this company prefix.

The first potential problem is that some customer enterprises—such as U.S. retailers—require potential vendors to submit their GS1 certificates as part of their certification package during the enrollment process, along with other information such as proof of insurance. The fact that "blocks of barcodes" were purchased means that the name on the GS1 certificate will not be the selling company—the company trying to be the vendor—but the company who owns the "blocks of barcodes" and this will likely not pass the inspection of the potential customer enterprise.

The next potential problem is that some U.S. retailers rely on GS1US' Data Driver for the creation of GTIN and related product information. The GS1US Data Driver is associated with a valid GS1US Company Prefix and account. When a block of barcodes are purchased from an independent reseller the buyer does not own the GS1 Company Prefix; allowing multiple manufacturers to use a single Data Driver account would expose each manufacturer to the other manufacturers' product information, and that in all likelihood includes full editorial control because the Data Driver accounts were never meant to be multi-manufacturer but rather associated with a single GS1 account. Any other item registry database that relies on the uniqueness of the GS1 Company Prefix could also be problematic for multiple purchasers of "blocks of barcodes."

Another potential problem is in the assignment of Global Location Numbers (GLNs). Formatted much like GTINs and supported by GS1 via their web site www.glnregistry.org, the purpose of the GLN "is used in electronic commerce documents to uniquely identify a legal entity, such as a whole company or a subsidiary, a functional entity, such as a purchasing department, or a physical location, such as a warehouse." If multiple manufacturers are using the same GS1 Company Prefix the registry in the GLN could be as compromised as that in the Data Driver: multiple manufacturers trying to use the same account. Compounding the issue, these multiple manufacturers could not use the same location identification serial number between them.

For example, manufacturers A and B which are both using Company Prefix 0123456 could not both assign location identifier 0010. How do isolated and unknown entities that each purchased "blocks of barcodes" coordinate with each other so they don't conflict on GLN identifiers? The ultimate answer is that they do not because they do not know about each other: the reseller is not going to coordinate this costly management effort nor give away the other block ownership information to the rest of the buyers for block self-management of GLN identifiers. Buying "blocks of barcodes" to assign to items does not address nor solve the location identifier issue.

Still another potential problem area is shipping container identification. The Serial Shipping Container Code (SSCC) is used to uniquely identify shipping cartons, master packs, and pallets. The main components of the SSCC are the two-digit application identifier, GS1 Company Prefix, serial identification number, and check digit. The serial identification number is just a serialized number, starting at zero and incrementing sequentially, not to repeat for up to one year from the date of the shipment between the shipper (vendor) and the receiver (customer). Multiple manufacturers sharing the same GS1 Company Prefix and—coincidentally sharing the same customer—would have to coordinate their assignment of the SSCC serial number to ensure none of the manufacturers (vendors) cross into the same range in use by any of the other manufacturer vendors shipping to the same customer. Just like the coordination of Global Location Number identifiers, this is an unrealistic task for both self-management of the buyers of the blocks of barcodes and the seller of the blocks of barcodes to perform.

Customer enterprises may decide to set as primary data fields in their ERP systems the vendors' GS1 Company Prefix identifiers for fast indexing and searching, and rely on the uniqueness of this data field. Given the widespread use of the GS1 Company Prefix across eB2B and auto-identification (inasmuch as only barcode labeling and scanning was mentioned the same data can be embedded in RFID tags) the potential for disruptive problems across different links of the supply chain are a real possibility, and in fact are more than likely in robust supply chains such as retail.

I submit that this level of coordination is ultimately unattainable because it relies on the independent reseller of the "block of barcodes" to continually coordinate with and advise the owners of shared company prefixes when a new purchaser has joined their group and all owners of the shared company prefix identifier must agree to align their ERP and eB2B systems to ensure no crossovers with each other's serial number ranges. Sharing GS1 accounts is unlikely going to be acceptable with each of the Company Prefix *users* as none of them are the rightful *owner*. None of the company prefix users can submit their GS1 membership credentials, (because none of the manufacturers are actually GS1 members), which are oftentimes (most notably in U.S. retail) required as part of the vendor compliance documentation.

Selling companies be forewarned: Only purchase your manufacturer identifier from GS1 or through the official government agency or designated trade association.

Is Vendor Compliance Worth It?

It is the dream of many companies—small, mid-size, and large—to grow their businesses by making the big leap into their respective industry's mainstream supply chains. But those dreams can quickly turn into expensive, money-losing nightmares if vendor compliance is not recognized up front and addressed as part of the decision.

At one client, already $50M in annual sales and a top-five national leader in their industry in the United States, I notified the company's chief executive officer before their meeting with a national retailer that his company was ill-prepared for the vendor compliance requirements and, due to the slim profit margins the company would likely lose money on their shipments. My client's technology and operations were simply not up-to-date and not coordinated to the point where I believed they could be successful in a national retail supply chain relationship. In a meeting with the company chief executive officer, vice president of operations, chief financial officer, and key department managers, I laid out my case and had the retailer's vendor compliance manual printed in front of me. When the executives began reviewing the myriad of requirements and the financial penalties they quickly understood my concerns, knowing their company's current limitations and operations. I was charged with the technology and operations improvements, and the relationship moved forward albeit on a smaller scale and with waivers for financial penalties (a rarity but still possible to negotiate sometimes). Within a few months after I formed a special team to handle eB2B orders and implemented updated eB2B software my client entered their national retailer partnerships with great success. And the eB2B orders team, which included customer service, distribution, and accounting members, out-performed the other employees fulfilling orders for non-eB2B customers in terms of throughput and accuracy such that they became the example by which the rest of the organization was to follow.

When approached with executive management support and dedication, vendor compliance will be a success. What the executives of my client knew was what I tell many of my clients considering vendor compliance: it is a considerable anti-competitive strategy. In some industries that have been slow to catch on to vendor compliance, early vendor adopters have been able to take advantage of forging close supply chain partnerships with their customers. But because of the necessity of vendor compliance to use it as a competitive weapon means more than just "being on board," for the vendor it means being smarter than their customer.

Vendors are in a position to receive sales or consumption data from their customers and to use this information to not only help manage their own businesses better but to also help their customer buyers by proactively communicating near to the next time a purchase order should be generated, or offering to send copies of sales or consumption analysis reports. Vendors should not assume that their buyers have easy access to report data or are not so inundated with information they have time to review it all; if the vendor enterprise can make life a little easier for their buyer, make the effort to do so. This collaborative spirit will help forge a closer supply chain relationship and may help grow the supply chain partnership, opening up new selling opportunities for the vendor with the customer enterprise.

But the vendor should not stop with just the one customer, because if the vendor can do all of this with one customer, the vendor can do all of this with any customer in the industry, and this can be a powerful incentive during a sales meeting. Showcasing the technology, operations, and analysis reports the vendor enterprise is capable of producing for its customers' buyers is a credential to the commitment of the vendor with regards to its dedication to vendor compliance and the spirit of the supply chain relationship. Buyers do not want to have to deal with a disruptive vendor: it only involves non-value added time and increases costs. Showcasing technology and operations and the results in terms of analytical reports that can be fed back to the buyer, if they desire, are a positive reflection on the vendor's savvy and desire for the customer's business.

Is vendor compliance worth it? For a business dedicated to doing it right, the answer is absolutely "yes." If you buy goods, be fair and ethical in the treatment of your vendors, and treat your vendors as meaningful as you treat your customers. If you sell goods, know that you are taking a great leap onto a path that will require dedication and investment, but the rewards can be well-within reach for companies willing to truly embrace what is required of them.

PART 4

Governing Ethically and Compliance Data Management

The Pros and Cons of Standards

Standards are a good thing: they provide uniformity with regards to how something is done; they set boundaries within which we are allowed to operate. Supply chain vendor compliance is all about the establishment of and adherence to existing standards, rules by which all vendors conduct business with a customer enterprise. So it should be a surprise to no one, to none of this book's readers that I am a big believer in defining standards and following the rules, which I am. But allow me to share with everyone, with all of my readers a little additional contrary insight:

Sometimes certain standards need to be avoided.

There are some supply chain standards that, in certain circumstances, are such an overwhelming burden for both the vendor and the customer to adhere to that common sense dictates that a more practical solution be used. This has traditionally been the case with the setup of item data.

The EDI Price/Sales Catalog (transaction number 832) or its EDIFACT counterpart transaction PRICAT is used to provide detailed item information to a trading partner, typically from a vendor to their customer. The contents of the EDI 832 contains information characteristic of a printed item price catalog:

- The item availability and expiration dates.

- Whether the item is new (added), being changed, or deleted.

- Minimum, maximum, or specific multiples order quantities.

- Item description.

- Pricing.

- Height, Width, Length, Volume, Weight.

- Packaging (e.g. the number of units in a master carton).

When I first entered the universe of supply chain vendor compliance in 1993, major U.S. retailers allowed vendors to submit standardized paper forms for item setup information in lieu of electronic transactions if the number of items was less than 50 or 100 depending on the retailer. Even with a data entry fee of $5US per item it was a much preferred method (and a better deal) rather than trying to establish the EDI 832 transaction and acquiring the data electronically from multiple sources. Sometimes it just pays to be practical. It was difficult enough for vendors to comply with the basic electronic business documents (e.g. the purchase order acknowledgement, invoice, and advance ship notice) that they had to send to the customer, so paying a small fee to avoid another electronic transaction was preferable.

When private electronic item catalogs began surfacing around several years later vendors selling a limited number of items could sometimes avoid this expense and effort as well, using the retailer's standard paper form (or by now also an electronic spreadsheet option) to submit the limited number of items for setup for the base per-item setup fee. These retailers generally understood that the expense and effort to establish a few items was not worth it for either the vendor or their own staff, and sometimes a simple paper form or spreadsheet was a better option. The private electronic catalogs were an awful expense: not only did a vendor have to pay to host their data, but a vendor paid for each customer trading partner who was granted access to the data.

Fast-forward a few decades and the private catalog I remember the most has been purchased and absorbed into larger companies: QRS® was bought by Inovis® in 2004 and then Inovis was acquired by GXS® in 2010. GS1US has their Data Driver® where products can be entered and barcode identifiers created; GLN Registry® for Global Location Numbers (e.g. the ship-from locations of vendor facilities); the GS1US Data Hub® where company, product, and location information can be stored. The terminology has been updated: today global supply chains speak of "data synchronization" and "pooling data," not just cataloging it, for "master data management" between customers and vendors, but the concepts are really no different, just the technology has improved.

From the outset you may be asking yourself what choices a vendor has if one customer trading partner required a certain item catalog and another customer trading partner required another item catalog. The vendor traditionally had no choice but to subscribe to both item catalog services, duplicating item information in both catalogs, doubling the amount of effort to maintain the same item information in both places, and increasing their item catalog costs. Whether the consolidation of item catalog services has helped at all today I am not sure though the benefit would be that a customer enterprise could easily subscribe to the top-two item catalog services and give their vendors a choice of which service to use. This would alleviate the necessity of a vendor established with one item catalog service from having to duplicate information (and expense) with another service. For the customer enterprise the ability to acquire data from the second catalog service should be no more difficult than adding a second set of predefined EDI 832 (or EDIFACT PRICAT) transactions from the alternate item catalog service provider.

Is this all even necessary for the vendor who just wants to sell a few items—or just one item—to its customer? That is the vendor compliance misadventure story that I am going to tell next. In giving away the answer to the aforementioned question the answer should be a resounding "No!" In fact as you will find requiring this vendor to stick to the standards was an exceptional waste of time and money for the vendor and consumed an exceptional amount of non-value-added time on the part of the buyer and buyer's assistant.

But as I sat down with my client to learn what they went through in their ordeal I was shocked to discover the egregious examples of unethical behavior exhibited by the customer enterprise, in this case a very large U.S. retailer, in their vendor management practices. What I had intended as a short standards story for the book would no doubt morph into a case of corruption and chaos equally well suited for my book on supply chain fraud. I will tell the tale and then recount the various essential elements that the retailer failed to uphold.

A Client Case Story

Names have been changed and certain details are not included so as not to disclose the identities of the supply chain trading partners and their related parties involved in the case story. All case story details are sourced solely from my client interview unless otherwise noted.

Clint, my client, had a product he wanted to sell to U.S. retail stores, and hired a sales representative who managed to get his company an audience with a buyer at a top-tier do-it-yourself retailer whose 2014 revenues exceeded $50BUS. The retailer buyer liked the product but suggested that there was no chance Clint's company could navigate the retailer's custom vendor compliance software systems and processes themselves, and that Clint's company should hire one of the retailer's preferred marketing partners for assistance. Clint stated that the suggestion was more of a recommendation, noting that the buyer effectively informed that no selling enterprise was able to provide their goods to the retailer without partnering with one of the retailer's preferred marketing companies.

Clint was introduced to BJ at Fast Partners, one of the retailer's preferred marketing companies. BJ it seems would be a good connection as he was a friend and neighbor of a former divisional vice president at the retailer, CB, who himself set up a company providing goods and services to the retailer after his retirement from there. With BJ's help Clint demonstrated the product at CB's house and, impressed with the product, CB was able to get Clint an audience with the retailer's CEO for a product demonstration who also was impressed with the product.

Inasmuch as Clint questioned the suggestion of working with a company recommended by the retailer he understood the rational of working with an entity with expertise: this is why companies hire consultants like me or those with specific legal, accounting, human resource, or other niche skills. As such Clint signed a contract with Fast Partners for 5 percent of sales with BJ informing that Clint's company just had to create the product codes necessary for barcoding the goods and his company would take care of the rest. Clint had experience creating retail product codes and selling to retailers and, with my expertise and guidance on the side for GTIN creation, began the process.

The first action Clint needed to take was to acquire an authorized manufacturer identifier from GS1, specifically GS1US because Clint is based in the United States. Membership in GS1US is based on a matrix predicated on the number of concurrent unique GTINs, and this information is available on the GS1US web site www.gs1us.org.

Clint then established his product and location codes. Recall that each GTIN represents a unique combination of product attributes (e.g. style, color, and size), and that each GLN represents a geographic location from which the customer enterprise may be interacting with the vendor, e.g. a vendor ship-from location. While this can be managed in a spreadsheet the Data Driver® product from GS1US offers to manage this information in their online toolset, which is what Clint did; in fact he had to in order to allow the data to flow through to the next link in the chain: 1WorldSync's Global Data Synchronization Network® (GDSN).

I mentioned independent data cataloging companies before, and 1WorldSync appears to be one of them. With the Clint's baseline product and location data stored in the GS1US Data Driver it could be extracted into the double-fee-based 1WorldSync GDSN product for synchronization to Clint's trading partners. (Clint informed that there was a sign-up fee and a fee for each customer trading partner that Clint would approve to access his company's information.) But that was not without the intervention of Idea4Industry (www.idea4industry.com), a company that as of March 2015 per their web site states: "As the official technology service provider and eBusiness standards body of the electrical industry ...," which is all well and good though Clint's company is not in the electronics industry business. Clint informs me that Idea4Industry's role is as the retailer's representative for 1WorldSync in the data synchronization process.

Unfortunately this is the point where serious subjective data issues began: the product packaging and product display configuration approved by the retailer was incompatible with the data setup within 1WorldSync's Data Driver. The product packaging agreed upon by Clint and the buyer would ultimately result in 35 pallets of product and display units, the display units in folded form ready for easy assembly. The 1WorldSync GDSN setup personnel informed that the retailer data setup would not accept such a product configuration and instead would require the displays to be shipped assembled with the products ready to install in the bottom, necessitating 700 pallets and requiring a lot of air to the shipped along the way.

(To put this in perspective, Clint informs that a standard size 53-foot truck trailer will hold between 26 and 30 fully cubed pallets with each pallet sized 40" × 48.").

Naturally Clint balks at the thought of shipping 20 times more pallets than the agreement with the buyer: aside from the insanity of shipping air in assembled product display stands, there is a higher risk of the assembled displays being damaged during the shipping processes, necessitating sturdier and therefore more expensive packaging and bracing materials, let alone just the overbearing cost of shipping 20 times more pallets would certainly be a deal-breaker from a vendor standpoint. Should the buyer have understood the data synchronization software systems restrictions? Good question.

Clint informs that nowhere was BJ or anyone from Fast Partners in providing insights or assistance in getting data set up. Clint began copying me on e-mails around the beginning of March 2014 preparing me for involvement. It was obvious from the e-mail communications that BJ and Fast Partners were actually washing their hands of any data setup responsibilities, claiming the retailer's systems and processes were just very difficult to maneuver. Really? An experienced company would be able to navigate even challenging software systems and business processes; Clint and I were both worried about the level of support Fast Partners was, or rather, was not, providing.

Clint's contact at Idea4Industry had identified that the data setup in 1WorldSync's GDSN would not be compatible with the retailer's own data management system. Against what would seem to make common sense and contrary to the advice of BJ and Fast Partners, Clint changed the product data setup in the GS1 US Data Driver which flowed through to the 1WorldSync GDSN for data pooling and synchronization to the retailer's own data management system, despite the fact that this data setup was now in stark contrast to how the buyer wanted the products established. What would the impact be to the purchase order? No purchase order had been generated yet, a fact that I will return to at the end of this story.

After repeated attempts the product and location data would not import—would not synchronize—to the retailer's system. At Clint's request I got more involved and reached out to the retailer buyer and was approved to access the retailer's systems. Clint also provided me his access to the GS1 US Data Driver. To resolve the subjective data disconnect I reviewed the data setup on both ends and worked with the buyer to try and get the data setup corrected. Over the course of four or five weeks I worked with the buyer and buyer's assistant to attempt to synchronize the product and location data, at one point exchanging 24 e-mails over the course of one 14-day period that also included several phone calls. The retailer's data management system was an unimpressive and undocumented abhorrence: a legacy mainframe system that was simply web-enabled with no obvious or common sense navigation to it. In fact on several occasions while on the telephone with the buyer, the retailer buyer herself struggled to understand and maneuver through her employer's own data management system.

Advising Clint on what I saw in the various systems and the feedback from the buyer he worked on changing the product and location data setups as necessary and finally was able to get both the product and location data synchronized in the retailer's system in the middle or late April 2014 timeframe and around a buyer-imposed deadline, too late for a Memorial Day holiday promotional launch as was originally planned but still in time for a July launch for the U.S. Independence Day holiday. However and unfortunately, and for no other reason, Clint suspects that the buyer's displeasure with Fast Partners and its failure to fulfill its obligation to help Clint's company be a vendor, the entire product launch was summarily canceled without another word.

THE FALLOUT

As I previously mentioned, at no time during this process was a purchase order submitted by the retailer, a rather wise move because a purchase order is a commitment to buy. Instead the retailer and the marketing company really just caused this selling company, Clint's company, to expend excessive resources to try and become a vendor to no avail. Clint's company had a product the retailer wanted and a product that the retailer's competitors—or at least main competitors—did not currently have. But cushy relationships, sweetheart deals, and unrealistic expectations scuttled what could have been a promising and profitable relationship for both trading partners.

The issues of the insider relationships are a problem. Tests for good governance should pose the question "Is this ethical?" Just because something is legal to do does not make it ethical to do. Determining if something is ethical should consider whether there is full disclosure and relative distance. Full disclosure means completely revealing relationship aspects if certain ties may potentially influence a decision, e.g. the buyer is the cousin or neighbor or is friends with a potential supplier. In this case the fact that former executives can—apparently with ease and approval—set up product and service companies with their former employer and seemingly lock in business, whether directly or indirectly, is a relationship that should not be able to exist. Relative distance means that—upon full disclosure—the person who may have a connection should not be involved in the determination of the relationship due to that person's closeness to the case. This "doing the right thing" is what making ethical choices is all about, and full disclosure and relative distance are two substantive and quite easy tests that can be applied.

The retailer, by allowing former executives to establish sweetheart deals after their retirement, using their former positions and contacts to their advantage, is likely legal but questionably ethical, especially if it goes as far as forcing prospective suppliers to use one of these companies or related companies in order to gain access to become a retailer supplier.

Clint informed me that these inside relationships seem to be standard, because at another top-tier do-it-yourself retailer of similar size he found the same self-serving structure: buyers pointing prospective vendors to use "preferred marketing companies" who were fronts for former executives or friends of former executives of the retailer who had established their own companies providing goods and/or services back to the retailer, sometimes displacing the retailer's own employees. Clint commented that this ultimately narrows the pool of vendors by blocking the field of prospective selling companies from the view of the buyers. It is unconscionable that Essential Element Ethics should be so blatantly stepped on, walked on, and disregarded in the name of lining the pockets of prior executives at the expense of the company's own fortunes. I will state again that vendor compliance is a strategy, not only for the vendor but also the customer. This retailer had the opportunity to one-up their competition with a unique product and they failed to take competitive advantage, instead their only perspective was the short-term and who on the inside could benefit the most.

What of all the data synchronization companies that were involved? Were they all necessary? Between GS1US, 1WorldSync, and Idea4Industry, only GS1US was a necessity because the products needed proper GTIN-12 (UPC) identifiers on them and the retailer required the establishment of GLN identifiers which are not unlike a GTIN in structure and are relatively easy to set up.

Remember: all of this was just to set up one product! Clint was providing the display cases and the products to fill them. Even the artwork and the Spanish-language translation services had to go through retailer-approved graphics and language translation companies, both of whom Clint informed failed to meet the retailer's requirements on the first run of their output and who both charged substantially more than Clint's preferred vendors.

It is unacceptable that a $50BUS company should leave in place and not redesign a web-enabled mainframe system that both its own employees and its vendors are left to suffer through. This smacks the Essential Element Educate right in the face. Neither the company's own employees could understand or explain (an Essential Element) this archaic system, let alone having it left up to the vendor community to deal with and rely on. This is not Essential Element Enablement, but rather the antithesis of it when systems are lazily left or low-prioritized because they are vendor-facing: not true as this story exposes, because the retailer's own employees (buyers) are actively engaged in the system and just as frustrated as the vendor community in trying to make sense of it and put it to use. At least the buyer was able to empathize (another Essential Element) with what we as a vendor were trying to accomplish in attempting to navigate their archaic software application as she struggled with it too. Unfortunately the empathy stopped there as this legacy application should have been scuttled and replaced ages ago. I would have to believe that if this was a consumer-facing application all resources would be dedicated to making it user-friendly and technically up-to-date, but because this application supported vendors it was likely left as a low-priority despite the fact that it was used by the retailer's own employees as well. As if an enterprise could exist without vendors and only customers/consumers: an enterprise needs both to survive. Both have a vital, critical role to play in the success of the enterprise, it is just that too rarely are they viewed as equally valuable.

What was attempted with a dysfunctional data chain could have been so easily satisfied with a form or spreadsheet and some data entry. In fact, the data entry could have been performed directly into the retailer's legacy data management system if such action would have been allowed, but that functionality was not permitted.

THE END RESULT

In the end, after the buyer scuttled the deal, Clint was left with nothing to show for his $100,000 in expenses (it would be inappropriate and inaccurate to use the term "investment") other than a costly education; 28,000 products he might be able to sell to discount stores for pennies on the dollar; and printed graphics and displays he may have to pay more money to have destroyed. What Clint does know is that he will build a minimum 25 percent markup into his future pricing before any other discussions with any other similar retailer.

There are few small companies, "small" being a relative word, that can easily afford to lose $100,000 dollars, (not that this is an easy loss for Clint), and still continue operations without a hiccup. (Clint's company generates a few million dollars a year in gross revenue.) But this begs the question as to how many $100,000 losses can Clint or any "small" company afford before they just stop trying to sell to big supply chain trading partners, e.g. top-tier retailers?

The unknown fees Clint—or any—selling enterprise may have to be aware of can include:

- Data management fees (e.g. 1WorldSync)

- Promotion or marketing company fees (e.g. Fast Partners)

- Displays and promotional materials (beyond what some selling enterprises might have been considering as normal in quantity and quality)

- Restricted use of graphics and translation companies and the services fees charged

- Barcode label approval services

- Shipping documentation (e.g. pack list, bill of lading) approval services

Beyond the fees and the 5 percent sales commission to the product marketing company for doing nothing else but managing a relationship that Clint and his sales representative were able to achieve on their own, Clint informed he would absolutely pay an expert (e.g. me) to manage the vendor compliance from the beginning for his next foray into big retail. Clint did not involve me at the beginning because he truly believed BJ and Fast Partners knew what they were doing at the outset but by the time he realized how bad things were, masked by BJ's incompetence, too much damage was done. I have known Clint since 1999 and have done several projects—small and large—for him over the years at his former company and now at his current company, which he owns. My reputation with him is sterling and he knows my expertise on this topic is unique. Sometimes too many cooks spoil the soup and I was cautious during the case to advise Clint and not step on BJ's and Fast Partner's feet until it was obvious that they were not doing their job which is when Clint asked me to be more engaged, though too late in the process to save the relationship with the retailer.

SOLUTION OPPORTUNITIES

I am not so wide-eyed optimistic to think that every entity (person or business) that has "the next big idea" is deserving of an audience with a retail buyer or buyer at a top-tier enterprise, e.g. government, automotive, aerospace, grocery, pharmaceuticals, etc. However, there are a few things that come to mind: First, enterprises do need to be on the lookout for the next disruptive or innovative idea or product and should open their eyes and ears more. Whether it is something anti-competitive or cost-saving, the next new idea could be a profit-generator and enterprises should integrate an entrepreneurial focus towards seeking out disruptive products and innovative technologies. Second, the qualification of the entity is a separate process from finding them. Perhaps the customer enterprise can help partner the idea entity with a manufacturer or distributor in order to bring the idea to fruition. Third, with all of the web-based technology available, somehow there must be a way to create a web portal for product and technology idea submission that would streamline the process. In retail for example, instead of hiding buyers behind walls open up opportunities by placing prospective products through a screening process of product specialists via a web-based submission. If the product passes the first step web review the selling enterprise would get the chance to send in a product sample for a physical review (if possible), and then a third step would be an invitation to meet with a product specialist or a buyer. A similar review process could be created for the submission of a technology idea to help local governments. The return-on-investment can be measured as to whether the needle-in-the-haystack product or idea revenue pays for the expense of operating the idea or product collection and review process. It may depend on the industry, but companies and government agencies have wasted far greater amounts of money on far more ludicrous and far-fetched schemes.

FOCUSED ON THE FUTURE

Retail in particular is facing a paradigm shift in how consumers interact with merchants, as shoppers shift from visiting brick-and-mortar stores to buying over the Internet to using mobile devices (e.g. smartphones) for price comparisons and store availability. This omnichannel environment is redefining how retailers approach the consumer experience and competition is fiercer than ever before as Internet-based retailers are successfully competing with traditional brick-and-mortar merchants and specialty retailers are losing out to multi-faceted department stores for commodity goods (e.g. office supplies, toys). Two-hour "last-mile" delivery to customers is being established by the likes of Amazon.com who also promises that drone aircraft will one day be delivering small packages to our doorstep. What will distinguish one retailer — online or down the street — from another? Price will most certainly differentiate commodity goods. Service — such as fast delivery — is stepping up as a separator but it remains to be seen whether it is financially viable. Definitely the challenges of stocking inventory, labor, fuel, and transportation times in traffic-choked locales present significant drawbacks to last-mile delivery within a one or two hour window. Customer service — the good old-fashioned face-to-face kind — still carries significant priority with many consumers and sometimes displaces price in determining where a consumer spends their money.

The one area where uniqueness can be carved out is in the product offerings. Once consumers get a sense that a retailer has what they want, and continues to offer products that other retailers (competitors) do not offer, consumers should put that particular retailer on their radar. With e-mail and social media marketing campaigns supporting traditional advertising promotions, any retailer offering unique products has the ability to really reach out and let their customer base know. But vendor compliance programs that do more harm than good—that cause enterprises to repulse rather than embrace prospective vendors—will only result in relegating those enterprises to remaining staid, stale, commodities in the eyes of their consumers.

Since 2001 I have operated a web site called www.vendorcompliance.info. True to its domain extension it is an informational place where a visitor can learn about supply chain vendor compliance and I have loaded the web site with useful links. I also receive a good number of inquiries from people with products and product ideas who ask how to get visibility to retail buyers. The advice I tell them is to build their own sales channel via a robust Internet site and to create a fan base using social media and customer relationship management. I tell them this because trying to get their innovative products in front of retail buyers is simply a dead-end proposition. At the end of each conversation the inquirer thanks me profusely for opening their eyes to new possibilities and saving them heartache and nightmares.

Inasmuch as I am not a retail merchandising expert, I can honestly say that some of the people who have contacted me have represented some quite clever products that I think select retailer buyers should have been interested in investigating. As the saying goes, there is, or should always be, room for a better mousetrap. And these people stated they had the supply chains to deliver or were able to ramp up to capacity when I questioned them on this.

The Internet is the great equalizer when it comes to the difference between separating commodity businesses and specialty sellers. Not everything has to be stocked on the store shelf when there is no limit to what can be available on the e-shelf. Maybe some retailers will innovate and open up a new online catalog area of innovative products and allow these entrepreneurs a chance once they pass through a qualification process. The retailer investment is likely moderate compared to the return and buzz it would generate among consumers.

Do not let supply chain vendor compliance be a blockade to innovating an enterprise's business model!

Compliance Data and Information Management

Whether the enterprise is a customer or a vendor, the implementation of vendor compliance requires the management of new data that will flow at minimum between the enterprise's ERP and eB2B systems with data translation in between. The capacity to manage—store, retain, dispose—of this data must be part of the conversation in the establishment of the vendor compliance program: how much, what kind, and for how long? The transformation of the data into meaningful—and actionable—information is dependent upon accurate analysis whereby customer miscalculations can result in the incorrect assessment of financial penalties or a misinterpretation can cause a vendor to lose out on a potential sale or up-sell opportunity.

BIG DATA CHARACTERISTICS

In tackling some of the issues surrounding the questions of data management, the characteristics of Big Data can provide a framework within which to begin addressing the fundamentals.

VOLUME

As I previously mentioned, in many or most supply chains the purchase order will be the initial transaction that occurs after the catalyst event happens that causes the supply chain to come into existence because the need to acquire something has occurred. This singular transaction can result in numerous other supply chain transactions: purchase order acknowledgement, purchase order change, routing request, routing instructions, advance ship notice, invoice, payment remittance, debit/credit adjustment. Some of these transactions, e.g. the purchase order and invoice, may reside in both the ERP and eB2B systems in their native and translated forms respectively. And let us not forget that with each of these transactions there will be a functional acknowledgement, though in my experience the number of characters in the functional acknowledgement is typically far less than that within the document transaction itself. The receipt of goods in the warehouse via automatic identification creates transactional data that may have heretofore not existed.

Whilst each of these transactions by themselves is analogous to a raindrop and individually, relatively, small in size, it is the incremental accumulation that causes massive floods. Because all of the transactions are related to the processing of an order, the retention of all of the transactions is necessary to form a complete picture of the full supply chain activity should research be required. This is even more important if track-and-trace requirements are part of the enterprise's supply chain in industries such as food, electronics, pharmaceutical, or chemical where lot, batch, or serial numbers would be included as part of the data communicated by the vendor. And therefore depending upon the industry the retention longevity may, in some cases, be many years while in other industries the necessary number of years may only be a few.

VELOCITY

Different links in the supply chain will move at different speeds, and the enterprise, whether the customer or the vendor, will have to adapt its systems and operations to the necessary speed at each link. Purchase orders may flow out of a customer enterprise at a moderate pace, and purchase order changes may be a rare occurrence. However for a vendor, the purchase order acknowledgement is generally required to be a 24-hour response, and this necessitates determining inventory allocation and quantities on hand and anticipated receipts from their suppliers for out-sourced activities. For vendors speed is of the essence in getting a purchase order acknowledgement turned around and done so accurately.

Receiving goods into a warehouse is another speed-related activity: goods are expected to be unloaded and checked in within a short timeframe. Conversely, the pick-and-pack process is often a time-intensive activity especially when compliance labeling, pallet stacking, and paperwork are added to the efforts. The typical requirement of the advance ship notice to be sent by the vendor within one hour of the shipment leaving the facility may be just about the most pressing of all time-sensitive vendor issues. The physical goods may sometimes move at a faster pace than the electronic documents themselves in many supply chains, though the electronic documents will always travel faster by their nature.

For customer enterprises that have ship-to (receiving) facilities in close proximity to its vendors' ship-from locations, there is a necessity to cycle the electronic mailbox receipt and data processing of the electronic ship notification (e.g. the EDI Advance Ship Notice) every 30 minutes. This would allow a vendor with a close-by facility sufficient time to have their electronic ship notification data processed before the goods physically arrive.

VARIETY

As indicated by the mention of the different transactions above, there will be a variety of data involved in vendor compliance. The purchase order can be acknowledged and changed; routing requested will be responded to with instructions; invoices will be associated with payment remittances and debit/

credit adjustments. For customer enterprises there may be different types of purchase orders depending upon the fulfillment requirement, e.g. bulk through a distribution center versus consumer direct drop-ship such as via a web site or catalog order. For vendors each customer enterprise will have its own unique set of data mapping, label format, and general vendor compliance requirements that must be incorporated into a single set of operational procedures and software systems. Variety is the nature of vendor compliance, and it is an ever-changing landscape of requirements.

And yet the variety is within standards that provide structure, enabling both the sender and receiver—the customer and the vendor—to work within established industry guidelines, e.g. ANSI X12, EDIFACT, and GS1. Not having to deal with unstructured data removes a significant burden and cost from the data translation process, and there is no concern about any meaning lost in translation. The supply chain data is effectively all character (text) based and is easily converted (mapped) from one format to another.

The reduction in the variety of data pertains not just to that within a standard but also across all data communicated to vendor trading partners, with the goal of delivering the data in the most usable format. Note that spreadsheets are not necessarily the most usable format though they may be the most user-friendly format. For the most practical purposes ancillary data (product sales, product forecasts, or product consumption) should be delivered in the same eB2B format (e.g. EDI, EDIFACT) as the transactional data is provided. This reduces the variety of data formats for the vendor and delivers the data in a format most conducive to mapping for integration to a business software application or database for retention and analysis. Translated as non-normalized data (as previously discussed), eB2B data can be easily imported into database applications and spreadsheets for analysis, with the mapping performed by either the vendor's translation software or data translation service provider. Therefore I believe it best that the customer enterprise should strive to deliver all of its data in the same (eB2B) format.

VERACITY

Depending upon which definition of "veracity" you go with, you can ask whether the data is truthful or the data is accurate. I think both are valid to address. With regard to truthfulness there should be little question as to the veracity of the data given that the customer enterprise initiated the data conversation with a trusted or qualified vendor. From the standpoint of accuracy, as I have previously reviewed, both the structure and the content of the transactions must be analyzed to ensure that there are no problems. The ERP system will perform its own business logic to protect against data entry errors. However the data mapping process in the conversion of the transaction from the ERP system to the eB2B system (whether the standard is EDI or EDIFACT) leaves the potential for error to occur. Auditing the eB2B converted data for integrity would be a wise move for both the customer and vendor before sending the transaction to the trading partner. Ensuring the truthfulness and accuracy of the data should be the responsibility of each trading partner; unfortunately in my experience I have discovered that it is more often left to the vendor to catch not just their errors but the mistakes of their customers as well, and suffer the consequences if they do not. Certainly validating the data even before it passes into the ERP system's business logic after it is mapped from the eB2B system is a wise move if the business logic layer of the ERP system is suspect or known to not be able to catch all of the potential data gaps that could exist.

RELEVANCY

All of the vendor compliance related data will be stored in the short-term, but what data should be retained in the long-term? In considering what data to retain—and for how long—the issue of how relevant the data is should be considered. An examination of the data with regards to it being relevant to other data and to any information goals are two key perspectives to undertake. Routing requests and instructions are important for vendor compliance performance because vendors are supposed to ship based on the instructions with which they are provided, but routing instructions probably have little relevancy for supplier risk analysis. Relevancy for the customer enterprise may impact how data is disseminated when different supply chain analysis is performed, e.g. performance versus risk. Relevancy for the vendor enterprise may determine who has access to the product activity data provided by the customers, especially if it is used as a check-and-balance against data in the vendor's own ERP system. Because the EDI Advance Ship Notice contains the UCC-128 carton and pallet barcode serial numbers and the contents of each carton, which may include serial numbered items or lot/batch identifiers and dates, retaining this information with related individual pallet or carton receipt scans may be beneficial if not also required, even though the excessive receipt scan data, while related, may also be redundant. Consider that the aggregation of data builds the profile of the target which in this case is the full lifecycle of the order. The more data retained for the timespan required the more evidence that exists if any questions arise, reducing knowledge gaps and confusion. Track-and-trace supply chains will likely need to retain the full range of supply chain data longer than other supply chains due to regulatory requirements.

The cost of data storage has to be weighed against the cost of time wasted on fruitless searches for missing information to research supply chain issues and the credibility lost with supply chain partners when vendor relationship personnel return empty results to vendor inquiries and cannot provide problem answers and resolutions. This is especially true when dealing with chargeback refutes by vendors. Remember that according to the Uniform Commercial Code (e.g. Article II Paragraph 515—Preserving Evidence of Goods in Dispute) the customer enterprise is responsible for the retention of evidence in support of the financial penalties it assesses upon its vendors. In modern supply chains this most certainly could—and arguably should—include the electronic data generated.

ONE SYSTEM OR MANY

Throughout the book I have focused on the necessity of the enterprise—the customer or the vendor—acquiring an Enterprise Resource Planning (ERP) system as its core business software application. This is a starting point or the minimum of what an enterprise should need from a business software perspective. Business can be complex, and one software application may not be sufficient. Enterprises sometimes operate multiple ERP systems across different acquisitions or divisions. When one software system does not have all of the features required to operate the business optimally, a best-of-breed approach whereby several software systems are selected, each specific to a functional area of the enterprise, and then integrated together may be implemented. Sales order processing, purchasing, warehouse management, accounting and finance, and electronic business-to-business functions can each be sourced from different software vendors who provide the "best" capabilities. (Also worth mentioning then is that bespoke applications developed by the enterprise internally or via an external provider are another avenue for acquiring the "best" or needed functionality, notwithstanding the return-on-investment decision.) Going back to the Big Data characteristic of Volume, consider that in a best-of-breed environment there may be a replication of transactions from one system to another, thus increasing the overall volume of data to be stored by the enterprise. For the purposes of simplicity throughout the book I have mentioned the functionality within a single ERP system knowing that in reality an enterprise may be operating multiple ERP systems or a best-of-breed environment. This does not change the conversation nor any facet of what makes up a well-run vendor compliance program from either a data or an operational perspective.

FOCUS ON THE FORMULAS

The cover story on the March 1, 2015 issue of *CIO* magazine (www.cio.com) titled "The New Math for CIOs" appropriately focuses on the point that decision-making algorithms run many systems and business leaders like CIOs need to understand them, even if it is the former rocket scientists and mathematicians who are deriving them.

"Almost every type of algorithm someone puts in place will have an ethical dimension to it. CIOs need to have those uncomfortable conversations." Michael Luc (assistant professor, Harvard Business School) *CIO* magazine, March 1, 2015.

The failure to get the formulas correct for the calculation of key performance indicators against a metric and the associated scorecard grades could result in vendors being unfairly charged financial penalties for non-compliance. Miscalculations or mistreatments of data (e.g. aggressive filtering or generous inclusion) that result in an incorrect analysis of vendor transactional data could incorrectly skew otherwise correct performance or risk calculations. So getting the formulas correct is not just about the mathematics, it is also about the query statements that cull the data before the formulas are applied.

"If algorithms are how you run your business and you haven't figured out how to regulate your algorithms, then by definition you're losing control of your business." Alistair Croll, consultant, author of "Lean Analytics: Use Data to Build a Better Startup Faster." *CIO* magazine, March 1, 2015

During my four-year involvement on the then-VICS TPAC committee I had some input into an already-started initiative called Trading Partner Performance Management (TPPM). A search on the GS1US web site (www.gs1us.org) for "Trading Partner Performance Management" will reveal this business requirements analysis document. The TPPM document contains the formulas—along with details—for key performance indicators Service Level Fill Rate, On-Time Delivery, Advance Ship Notice Pack List Accuracy, On-Time Advance Ship Notice Delivery, Pre-Ticketed Product Accuracy, Packaging Specifications Accuracy, and Carton Label Accuracy. While some of these are clearly related to the retail industry specifically, several of these calculations could be applied to almost any industry. These calculations were carefully reviewed by the TPAC committee members as were the associated terms and definitions. Just like my belief that industry-supported vendor education is the best way and is what trade associations should be promoting with support of their members, similarly these same types of efforts—the definition of standard terms and calculations—helps to take the confusion and chaos out of the customer-vendor relationship, making the trading partnership more equitable and ethical.

RISK AND REWARD

The common use of the data collected in a vendor compliance program is to analyze vendor performance and produce the vendor scorecard, integral components of a supplier relationship management initiative. These same data points can also be used for a supplier risk management program to ascertain whether a supplier is on the brink of failure. While there are other attributes that must be considered in a supplier risk profile, and even before a selling company is engaged in a trading partnership, it is the ongoing monitoring (a COSO framework concept, something I will review later in this part of the book) of transactions and the analysis of a pattern that indicates a potential vendor failure or, for that matter, fraud as I discussed in my book *"Detecting and Reducing Supply Chain Fraud"* (Gower, 2012).

The same initiatives by customer enterprises that are trying to drive high efficiencies and margins might be having a whiplash effect when it comes to pushing their vendors to compromises.

In their 2014 whitepaper titled "Supply Chain Management Challenges" Thomson-Reuters Accelus highlights 10 supply chain management obstacles which, according to the whitepaper, are primarily due to a "lack of management, transparency, and monitoring" and less due to complexities in the supply chains themselves, even as supply chains are stretched globally. (I could certainly make the case that much of this book is about the management of the vendor relationship, transparency in the vendor relationship, and monitoring the vendor relationship transactions in terms of performance analysis, risk analysis, and fraud detection.) The seventh challenge on the list states: "As suppliers are squeezed on costs and tight delivery schedules, they may be enticed to cut corners. This can result in quality problems which can have significant knock-on effects throughout the supply chain." Customer enterprises must be cautious about making themselves so overly efficient that they place themselves in a higher risk category. There must be a balance between efficiency and practicality in the relationship between supply chain operations and supply chain risk. This harmony not only affects the customer enterprise but most certainly significantly impacts the customer's vendor community as well.

I previously cautioned about implementing "too much too fast" when it comes to customer enterprises and the expectations of their vendor community. The unintended consequences beyond just dealing with unhappy vendors and potential delays in full acceptance with vendor compliance initiatives become clearer now as it may lead to greater risk in what could already be a vulnerable supply chain. Empathizing with your vendors—an Essential Element—is not to be mistaken as a capitulation or compromise in the vendor compliance requirements. Take it as the opportunity before the requirements are released to consider if the requirements make common sense, are explained clearly, provide all the data and information necessary for implementation, and are overall achievable for the vendor community. In a requirement being "achievable" consider that it must be affordable and available (easily acquirable) by the vendor community at large. Ensure that your vendor compliance implementation does not backfire and result in more disruption to your supply chain than what may already exist.

As noted in the February 2013 whitepaper by the Supply Chain Risk Leadership Council (www.scrlc.com) titled "Emerging Risks in the Supply Chain," point number two ("Global, JIT, Lean Supply Chains"), business models that reduce inefficiencies can also produce single points of failure. Without a balance the disruption of a single supply chain link can cause the entire chain to break. Thorough analysis of the supply chain activities end-to-end can help determine where breaking points might occur and possibly predict damaging activities, such as overloading capacities, before they happen.

The data analysis of the supply chain information should be an introspective perspective as well to ascertain whether the customer enterprise is pushing their vendors too hard and therefore if the customer enterprise is heading towards causing their own supply chain catastrophe. Analyzing vendors for performance and risk patterns is fine, but the root cause may find the fault lies ultimately with the customer enterprise in the overly aggressive or haphazard implementation of vendor compliance initiatives.

INFORMATION COLLABORATION

In their August 2011 whitepaper titled "Supply Chain Management: A Compilation of Best Practices," the Supply Chain Risk Leadership Council notes specifically that the supply chain risk management team should include representation from, among other functions such as finance, governance, logistics, manufacturing, and procurement, the supplier management function.

This organization recognizes the collaboration between supplier relationship management and supplier risk management.

I take this collaboration farther since the set of data the enterprise has at its disposal is fixed, consigned to the data it generates or the data it receives from its trading partners. As such this data must be shared cooperatively across different functions for different purposes to maximize its use, e.g. both supplier relationship management for performance analysis and supplier risk management for risk analysis. (I could also add another use as in fraud analysis based on my detecting and reducing supply chain fraud business model.) Whilst other factors (financial, geo-political) contribute to a vendor's risk profile, performance analysis over time can certainly be a telltale sign.

While examining data for supplier performance and supplier risk, the data generated by and received by the enterprise can also be analyzed to ascertain internal risks such as capacity limitations like inventory storage shortage, labor shortage, dock space limitations, or manufacturing constraints. A review of the volume of transaction data and by scanning the content of the transactions and aggregating the detail, (e.g. item quantities, weights, and volumes), will reveal patterns of consistency, increase, or decrease and allow the enterprise to react accordingly.

BUILD IT OR BUY IT

How can or should an enterprise approach tackling the analysis of this data and ensuring it is transformed into accurate and meaningful information, now that it is more clear the significant impacts to supplier performance and risk analysis, fraud detection and internal risks, and the ethical consequences involved.

Having progressed in my career beginning as a software developer, something I still do from time to time, there are certainly still those instances when a custom application is required because the right solution is not available (does not exist or is not attainable, e.g. too expensive). However I am a big proponent of buy it if you don't have to build it: why recreate the proverbial wheel if you do not have to, if it already exists?

Just slapping dashboard software over the top of an ERP system is not going to provide the desired solution. The data has to be set up conducive to the outcome, supporting both the business transactions and the business analysis. Transactions must be balanced to ensure an entire process is encapsulated, e.g.

an electronic ship notice along with the electronic data capture of the inbound goods which is one way of determining carton label accuracy. (If carton label identifier barcodes are not present in the advance ship notice, and conversely there are carton identifiers in the advance ship notice that are not received, the mismatch, in lieu of any theft, is one example of an accuracy problem.) The mathematical formulas used to determine the key performance indicators must be derived, preferably from standards either within or outside the enterprise's own industry. The setting of the scorecard or dashboard value of the key performance indicator must be established and fine-tuned as conditions change. Are vendors who fall below 90 percent compliance a problem? Perhaps not in the beginning of a vendor compliance program rollout, but maybe one year into the initiative. Who determines these settings or does some system automatically make the adjustments based on some criteria under parameters set and controlled and reviewed by whom and how often and triggered by what set of circumstances (e.g. transaction volume passes a certain level)?

SUMMARY

As the saying goes, "the devil is in the details" and this is certainly true for the setup of software systems and the expectations of the information that they produce. Objectively the attributes of the data will determine if the software system is the best choice: if the demands of the data require more fields than the software provides, the system in its current state is insufficient. Subjectively, how the characteristics of the primary business entities—customers, items, and vendors—are established will eventually determine how the business transactions can be analyzed and what information will be available upon which to make strategic decisions, and the ease or difficulty of eB2B data mapping and integration.

Implementing vendor compliance increases the amount of data an enterprise will generate and ultimately should retain for analysis: data storage is rather affordable these days so my recommendation is do not be stingy and retain what is sufficient to perform trend analysis, support chargeback assessments (for customer enterprises), and challenge chargeback assessments (for vendor enterprises). Using the attributes of Big Data as a guide estimating the amount of storage capacity and growth are both achievable exercises.

Much like I promoted in my supply chain fraud business model, let the data generated and collected in a supply chain vendor compliance program have at least a dual-purpose: performance analysis and risk analysis, though its use for fraud detection and internal capacity risks is achievable with the data being available. Regardless of whether your enterprise is a customer or a vendor, data is being generated and collected and is ripe and ready for use. Do not let the opportunity for insight pass you by: understand what data you have available to you and then understand how it can be used strategically.

Whether you decide to build or buy or some combination of both, make sure the solutions you implement to analyze your data are based upon carefully thought-through formulas. Do not just let some software developer or information technology professional decide what the calculation should be: this is a management-level decision involving input from senior executives with different perspectives. Incorrect arithmetic can result in significantly negative consequences that can strain trading partner relationships due to false accusations or cause financial damages due to poor strategic investment choices. Check your math and then double-check your math!

Governing Ethically

In July 2002 the Sarbanes-Oxley Act, also known by its nickname "SOX," was passed by the United States federal government in response to the collapse of several public companies due to shenanigans by their chief executives. The company implosions resulted in massive job losses and the implications were felt throughout the stakeholder community, e.g. service and product vendors. SOX is not just about the timely and accurate reporting of financial statements, it is also about how those accurate and timely financial statements are achieved. In other words, the process matters as much as the results. One of the most commonly used SOX compliance frameworks is produced by the Committee of Sponsoring Organizations (COSO) of the Treadway Commission (www. coso.org). According to its web site, COSO was formed in 1985 "to sponsor the National Commission on Fraudulent Financial Reporting." Its mission is to provide guidance and thought leadership in three areas: risk management, internal control, and fraud deterrence, with a goal of improving organizational performance.

Let me jump for a moment to the supply chain and my definition: *The movement of something between a supplier and a customer from start to finish.* What moves can be anything: data, information, raw materials, documents, components, finished goods, people, services, or money. From start to finish means that the movement is in one direction, from the supplier to the customer, and should be performed one time and with completion. (To have to return something from the customer to the supplier and repeat a step would typically indicate a quality failure of some kind.) The customer-supplier relationship can be internal to the enterprise, external to the enterprise, or a mixture of internal-external. An internal relationship would be that of the human resources department as a supplier of services to the employees, or the information technology department as a supplier of goods and services to the whole of the enterprise. Other examples of internal customer-supplier relationships are inventory to manufacturing, and quality control to inventory. A relationship external to the enterprise may be one where a vendor provides goods or services to a customer and the enterprise is managing the exchange, such as in the case of retail where goods are drop-shipped from the manufacturer or distributor directly to the consumer and are never handled by the retailer. An internal-external relationship is one where an external supplier is providing goods or services to the customer enterprise. The point is that different relationships exist for the enterprise and internal supply chain relationships are just as abundant, though perhaps less obvious, than external or internal-external supply chain relationships.

Vendor compliance concepts can be applied to internal supply chain relationships just as they can be applied to internal-external and external supply chain relationships: each of the Essential Elements is necessary if the inner-workings of an enterprise are going to function effectively, just like if a vendor compliance program is going to be successful. The goals of the enterprise do not change whether the supply chain relationships are internal or external or a mixture of the two, and neither should any expectation in quality or performance of those involved, (employees or vendors), in powering the engine that drives the enterprise forward.

Inasmuch as SOX is legally applied to only U.S. public companies, private enterprises and those outside the United States should take note of what SOX compliance frameworks have to offer in their guidance. Successful supply chain vendor compliance, characterized by the Essential Elements I have identified, fits very nicely into the COSO compliance framework's five key aspects. I bring these two concepts together to dispel any notions that vendor compliance cannot—or should not—be used internally or that it should take a back-seat because it contains the word "vendor," not "customer."

CONTROL ENVIRONMENT

The control environment is also known as the "tone at the top." It is the personality, if you will, of the enterprise as set by the words and actions of executive management. If this moral compass is pointed straight and true, the enterprise will act with good character towards its stakeholders: employees, customers, vendors, and investors. If its moral compass is askew the best interests of the stakeholders are cast aside and the interests of the executives are self-serving.

Executive management, in setting the tone, must place the importance of vendors equal to the value of customers: they are an equal stakeholder in the enterprise. (I will add the ethical tone certainly extends to prospective vendors as well.) Resources must be dedicated to the vendor compliance program on a comparable scale such that the program will succeed, e.g. the right software and hardware technology investments are made, the right employees are hired and trained.

The ethical tone of the enterprise should prohibit insider deals with current or former executives in the provision of goods and services, especially if it restricts prospective vendors to utilize the services of selected "marketing" companies in order to gain access to buyers or to complete the deal. Note that my client already had a meeting with the buyer and the buyer wanted the product my client had proposed. Unfortunately the buyer was unable to close the deal without my client utilizing one of the retailer's marketing service companies to supposedly, purportedly, guide them through the technical and operational requirements process.

Further, the customer enterprise should not unethically use chargebacks— the financial penalties for non-compliance—as leverage in vendor deals to sweeten contract terms in order to acquire sought-after brands. All vendors should be treated the same and this includes equal punishment under the customer enterprise's laws. More egregious, if the chargebacks are used as a profit center, profiting off the backs of the smaller vendors while giving the larger more profitable vendors a pass, whether contractually stated or wink-of-the-eye understood, is even more ethically unbalanced. Nor should financial penalties be excessive beyond what is reasonable, what is ethical, and what is legal.

RISK ASSESSMENT

The risk assessment examines all risks to the enterprise, regardless of whether the source of the risk is internal or external. Vendor compliance programs, in their ability to measure vendor performance through the vendor scorecard, can aide in the vendor risk assessment profile. The vendor enrollment process can help to mitigate the risk of establishing an initial relationship with a questionable company, though it is the longer-term relationship that is likely to be where the risk resides. In my book *Detecting and Reducing Supply Chain Fraud* (Gower, 2012) I discuss how supply chain technologies ERP, EDC, and eB2B can be used together to detect and reduce fraud by cross-examining the transactional information. This continual monitoring (a COSO framework aspect) of the transactional information and cross-checking for potential fraud is a risk-mitigation plan, a fraud detection and reduction business model, that has at its foundation the implementation of supply chain vendor compliance.

CONTROL ACTIVITIES

Whether you refer to them as policies and procedures, approvals and authorizations, or checks and balances, these are the rules that limit what can be done. In a broader sense the vendor compliance documentation represents the control activities that define, for a vendor, what can and cannot be done within the vendor's interaction with the customer enterprise. The general vendor compliance manual outlines what activities are and are not permissible, e.g. child labor laws and gift policies, as well as expectations on eB2B interactions. The data mapping guide dictates what data will be expected to be exchanged back and forth by document (transaction). The routing guide defines which transportation carriers to use under what circumstances, e.g. shipment weight and ship-to destination.

Defined internally, control activities can be considered the standard operating procedures of the enterprise: how things are done based on a specific business scenario occurring. Defined are who is involved, what are the processes involved, what software systems are involved and the function used, and what happens if something goes wrong.

INFORMATION AND COMMUNICATION

This aspect of COSO can be summarized as "Who needs what information and when it is it needed?" Without the proper—and accurate—information people cannot effectively perform their jobs. The right people need the right information at the right time in order to make the right decision. (This sounds like the Customer Bill of Rights I referred to earlier, doesn't it?) The "right people" includes vendors, as well as customers and employees. Vendors must be assured of receiving the right information at the right time so that they can react and deliver the right goods at the right place at the right time. Providing vendors timely and accurate purchase orders, product sales data, forecasts, and scorecard results only aides in their ability to execute, whether it is to respond with a transaction or correct a performance issue.

For the vendors, they need to provide the right information, e.g. purchase order acknowledgements, advance ship notices, and invoices, at the right time to the customer enterprise to ensure that the supply chain, in its information and product movement, is not interrupted and kept flowing smoothly.

MONITORING

This aspect of COSO checks for the accuracy, adherence, effectiveness, and relevancy of the other aspects. It does no good to implement a software system or business process if it does not produce accurate output, is not adhered to, is not effective in fixing the problem it was intended to, or is not relevant to the problem it was supposed to fix.

In terms of vendor compliance, the monitoring activity certainly applies to the vendor scorecard and the performance oversight of the vendors. But the monitoring activity should also be watchful over the entire vendor compliance program to ensure its elements remain adhered to, are effective, and are relevant. If vendors are not adhering to a particular requirement, the reason why should be sourced. Was the requirement unreasonably difficult or unattainable to comply with, e.g. was the necessary technology required very expensive to acquire? If a vendor compliance requirement is no longer effective in solving a problem, e.g. colored packing tape or colored labels as visual indicators, then remove the requirement right away and reduce the burden on the vendor community. If a compliance requirement has lost is relevance, e.g. a technology has become outdated, a tag is no longer required, then remove the requirement and alleviate the requirement from the vendors. The continual monitoring of the vendor compliance program includes feedback from the vendor community: this can be either solicited via surveys or unsolicited via input from the vendor relations team based on their interactions with the vendor community or through comment postings if the enterprise has a vendor portal that permits such interaction, though most vendors would be reluctant to post for fear of identity discovery and retribution. Nonetheless, a truly anonymous feedback feature would likely generate some great honest insights about some of the deep-rooted problems with the vendor compliance program. However, based on my experience I have never encountered a customer entity that cared what their vendors thought about their vendor compliance program or the dysfunctional issues within to solicit feedback like this, which I find rather unfortunate and short-sighted.

THE HEART OF THE MATTER

Vendor compliance sits at the core of supplier relationship management. The ability to define the relationship with another entity is one of great responsibility, and this power should not be abused. Leveraging one's might is intoxicating but it does not make it right, and it is tempting when one is themselves trampled upon but perpetuating a problem does not make it go away or correct itself. Ethical behavior matters. Empathy is not a weakness. Rules that apply to one should apply to all. Relative distance and full disclosure should not just preclude but exclude insider deals that are more focused on short-term gains for a few than the long-term goals of the customer (or vendor) enterprise. Vendors are just as valuable as consumers and the smart customer enterprise knows this and embraces this concept.

Supplier risk management programs can use the results of vendor compliance scorecards to assist in ascertaining if a vendor is becoming a risk. Performance is not the only risk characteristic, e.g. geographic location is another, but certainly how the vendor is performing across a variety of metrics is a strong indicator of the vendor's stability or instability. Therefore the ability of the customer enterprise to accurately ascertain a vendor's guilt in its failure to comply with a compliance requirement is of the upmost importance. As I quote Peter Parker's (a.k.a. Spiderman) Uncle Ben who said "With great power comes great responsibility," as the customer enterprise acts as judge, jury, and executioner in solely determining the vendor's conformity to vendor compliance requirements, the customer enterprise has to be perfect in their own performance and ability, including mathematical calculations, to make this determination. If the customer enterprise cannot accept this responsibility it is only ethically fair that a compromise system be put in place which accepts that to err is human for both the customer and vendor alike.

The customer enterprise should also use the supply chain data collected to determine if it is causing itself harm in stressing its capacities, e.g. labor, facility space, throughput, to their limits. The cross-examination of transactions from different supply chain systems is a strategy for detecting and reducing fraud. In both cases the ability to examine trends and possibly predict outcomes enables the enterprise to prevent or mitigate problems early on. It is an exceptional return-on-investment from the same data being used to operate the supply chain and analyze vendor performance.

The technologies used in vendor compliance, notably Enterprise Resource Planning systems, Electronic Data Capture, and Electronic Business-To-

Business may be decades old but are more relevant and reliable today than ever before; without these technologies supply chains like retail simply could not function, certainly nowhere near to the demands or expectations of the consumers. I have heard these technologies referred to the lifeblood of robust supply chains. (With regards to Electronic Data Capture: barcode labeling and scanning is definitely decades old while radio frequency identification is much more recent. However radio frequency identification is nowhere near as yet pervasive in supply chain use as the ubiquitous barcode label at this point, so I am really referring to the barcode label here rather than more current up-and-coming technologies like radio frequency identification.)

Supply chain vendor compliance is a strategy for both the customer and vendor. For the customer enterprise, vendor compliance is a way of improving operations and reducing costs due to inefficiencies which come with not having standard operating procedures. However, some of those inefficiencies will be lost and costs will increase with poorly run vendor compliance programs that require excessive oversight and vendor management as the result of ineffectively implemented technologies and guidelines, confusing documentation (guides, web sites), and uneducated customer enterprise staff and vendors resulting in frustrating communication disconnects and repeatedly asked questions answered differently each time.

For customer enterprises vendor compliance is an anti-competitive strategy that should enable the acquisition of new technologies or new products which result in differentiating the customer from its competitors in the eyes of its consumers. Some businesses have simply become commodities to consumers, especially I believe true in retail, so companies will have to innovate to compete on something other than discounted prices. Whether the item is found on the store shelf or e-shelf, the customer enterprise that can bring new products to consumers is the one that will generate the greater sales.

For selling companies vendor compliance represents a major leap in persona change to being a vendor, and the myriad of operational and technical changes (responsibilities) that come along with the transformation are significant. Without executive management support the selling company has little to no chance of success, thus the *control environment* ("tone at the top") is critical from the outset. For selling companies, but also for customer enterprises seeking to re-examine their processes and systems, vendor compliance is an introspective perspective into how things are done and how things will be performed as the bar is raised to meet the high expectations of the selling company's top-tier customers or the customer enterprise's top competitors and consumers.

Tradition is history: how things were done in the past no longer matters. New business procedures and new technologies, staff education and training, and a commitment to the "perfect order" is all that matters in accepting the role of a vendor. It is an anti-competitive strategy that separates the selling company from its competitors. And the smart vendor, using the data provided by its customers, will analyze this collected data to return information to its own management to make better strategic decisions, and to its own sales personnel to make them more effective at their next buyer meeting. The smart vendor will use the data at hand to try and be as smart, if not smarter, than their customer. This is how vendor compliance can help conquer the competition.

CLOSING COMMENTS

The value of even the smallest vendor should never be overlooked. Since January 1996 my one-person company Katzscan Inc. (www.katzscan.com) has been providing technical and management advisory services to enterprises that have ranged in size from $5M to $1.5B in gross annual sales, with some companies being U.S. national, if not sometimes international, leaders in their respective fields. I have consulted CEOs, CFOs, CIOs, and vice presidents on business strategies and tactics, turning around and inside-out their perceived problems and driving into the data and operations for solutions. I have written mission-critical software that produced millions of barcode labels, mapped data between software systems, analyzed millions of data records to produce meaningful information, converted data, enabled millions of dollars of business to be transacted, have created business software applications to perform various mission-critical business functions, and implemented and worked with various ERP and eB2B/EDI solutions. I work to create a closer trading partnership between my clients and their suppliers, mindful of the vendor compliance requirements the supplier is asked to do. I act as the liaison between my clients and their largest customers, forging and strengthening the operational and technical supply chain trading partner bonds between them. Yes, even the smallest vendor can have the biggest impact on an enterprise.

Sometimes relationships are one-and-done, sometimes relationships do turn sour. Supply chains—whether internal or external or a mix of both— are all about relationships, whether between departments, business units, or trading partners. Sometimes what supply chains need is just some good old fashioned counseling: someone to listen to what the partners involved are each saying and to help everyone come to an equitable resolution. Yes, I perform that service as well.

Relationships matter and this has never been truer than in supply chain partnerships. Without taking unfair advantage these relationships can be leveraged so that both parties—the customer and the vendor—can benefit. But this can only happen if the lead party—the customer—starts out the relationship the right way, and continues to grow the relationship equitably. I think that most customer enterprises would read into this that fair and equitable equates to lost revenue, but I am adamant that is not true. The cost of operating most vendor compliance programs is out of control due to how poorly they are managed, and financial penalties for non-compliance (a.k.a. chargebacks) should not be a profit center. These are the signs of an abusive relationship, not a healthy relationship.

Value your vendors just as much as you cherish your customers.

Online Resources

Accredited Standards Committee
Available at: http://www.x12.org/

American National Standards Institute
Available at: http://www.ansi.org/

Committee of Sponsoring Organizations of the Treadway Commission
Available at: http://www.coso.org/

Cornell University Law School – Legal Information Institute – Legal Dictionary
and Encyclopedia
Available at: http://www.law.cornell.edu/wex

Cornell University Law School – Legal Information Institute – Uniform
Commercial Code
Available at: http://www.law.cornell.edu/ucc

EDItEUR
Available at: http://www.editeur.org/

GS1
Available at: http://www.gs1.org/

GS1-UK
Available at: https://www.gs1uk.org/

GS1-US
Available at: http://www.gs1us.org/

GS1US – Global Location Number (GLN) Registry
Available at: http://www.glnregistry.org/

Idea 4 Industry
Available at: http://idea4industry.com/

IDG Enterprise / CXO Media
Available at: http://www.cio.com/

Katzscan Inc.
Available at: http://www.katzscan.com/

Katzscan Inc.
Available at: http://www.vendorcompliance.info/

Material Handling and Logistics
Available at: http://mhlnews.com/global-supply-chain/customers-bill-rights

National Marine Manufacturers Association
Available at: http://www.nmma.org/

National Motor Freight Traffic Association
Available at: http://www.nmfta.org/

PCI Security Standards Council
Available at: https://www.pcisecuritystandards.org/

Supply Chain Risk Leadership Council
Available at: http://www.scrlc.com/

The National Conference of Commissioners on Uniform State Laws
Available at: http://www.uniformlawcommission.com/

United States Census Bureau – North American Industry Classification System
Available at: https://www.census.gov/eos/www/naics

US Legal, Inc.
Available at: http://www.uslegal.com/

Voluntary Interindustry Commerce Solutions
Available at: http://www.vics.org

Wikipedia
Available at: http://en.wikipedia.org/wiki/X12_EDIFACT_Mapping

Index